GERM
MO

CW00867514

Volume 1
Steam, Electric, Battery
& Departmental Vehicles

1st Edition

Neil Webster

ISBN 0-947773-23-1

Typeset by StreetWise, 18 North Terrace, Birstall, Batley, West Yorkshire WF17 9EU

FOREWORD

The re-unification of Germany has in railway terms lead to the development of a situation unique in Western Europe, whereby the major part of the railway system is operated by two seperate enterprises, both of whom are owned by the state. In the former eastern section of the country services are operated by the Deutsche Reichsbahn (DR) and in the former western section by the Deutsche Bundesbahn (DB). How long the two will remain seperate entities in the future remains to be seen, as progressively they are coming closer together, with loans of rolling stock and other resources between the two operators now being commonplace.

A unified system of numbering of the locomotive and multiple unit fleets of the two operators was announced during 1991, to take full effect as and from 1st January 1992. This largely affects the numbers carried by DR vehicles, although a few DB vehicles have also been affected. For the first time in an english language publication the two volumes of this book list the complete fleets of Locomotives and Multiple Units of both the DB and DR in one publication, together with their former numbers (prior to 01.01.92) if applicable and also depot allocations. Details are as far as possible updated to the autumn of 1991, but readers are asked to submit details of any additional or amended information which may come to light to the author via the publishers address shown on the title page.

Neil Webster
February 1992.

NOTES

DETAILS & DIMENSIONS

For each vehicle type brief technical details are given in metric units. Weights given are those in working order with a full complement of all necessary supplies (e.g. fuel and water). Lengths quoted are over buffers/couplings as applicable. Codes are used to indicate the various builders/manufacturers/constructors and these are common throughout both volumes of this work. Details of these codes are given in a table at the beginning of each volume. Abbreviations used for metric units follow the internationally accepted standards and are as follows:

kg	kilogrammes
kg/cm²	kilogrammes per square centimetre
km	kilometres
km/h	kilometres per hour
kW	kilowatts
m	metres
mm	millimetres
rpm	revolutions per minute

LOCOMOTIVE & MULTIPLE UNIT NUMBERING SYSTEM

Each vehicle is allocated a six digit number, followed by a computer check digit. The first three digits of the number denote the class, and the second three digits the serial number of the vehicle. The first digit of the number denotes the type of vehicle as follows:

0 - Steam Locomotive.
1 - Electric Main Line Locomotive.
2 - Diesel Main Line Locomotive.
3 - Shunting Locomotive/Tractor.
4 - Electric Multiple Unit.
5 - Battery Electric Multiple Unit.
6 - Diesel Multiple Unit.
7 - Departmental Vehicle or Diesel Railcar.
8 - Electric Multiple Unit trailer.
9 - Diesel Multiple Unit or Railcar trailer.

The second and third digits of the number are used to differentiate between the different types of vehicle within a type of traction. An exception to this is with regard to narrow gauge vehicles, where the second and third digits of the number are always 99, irrespective of the vehicle type.

The fourth, fifth and sixth digits of a standard gauge vehicle and the fifth and sixth digits of a narrow gauge vehicle denote the individual vehicle serial number. For narrow gauge vehicles the fourth digit indicates the gauge of the vehicle as follows:

1 - 1000 mm gauge.
6 - 600 mm gauge.
7 - 750 mm gauge.
9 - 900 mm gauge.

In the case of multiple unit trailer vehicles, non-driving trailers are always allocated serial numbers between 001 and 599, and driving trailers between 601 and 999.

The seventh digit is a computer check digit used to verify that an entry made to the railway computer is correct. These digits are actually carried on the vehicles, but are not shown in this book. The computer check digit may be calculated for any vehicle as follows:

(155 236)	1	5	5	2	3	6
Multiply by	1	2	1	2	1	2
Answer	1	10	5	4	3	12

Sum of digits of answer = 1+1+0+5+4+3+1+2 = 17
Subtract from next whole multiple of 10, viz 20-17 = 3
Check digit for 155 236 is thus 3.

GUIDE TO VEHICLE/EQUIPMENT BUILDERS

Note: All builders are German unless otherwise stated.

23rd August	"23rd August" Works, Bucharest, Romania.
ABB	ASEA Brown Boveri Transportation AG, Mannheim.
AEG	Allgemeine Elektricitäts Gesellschaft, Berlin.
AFA	Akkumulatoren-Fabrik-Hagen, Hagen.
Bautzen	VEB Waggonbau Bautzen, Bautzen.
BBC	Brown, Boveri & Cie AG, Mannheim.
BEW	Bergmann-Elektrizitätswerke AG, Berlin.
Borsig	Borsig-Lokomotivwerke GmbH, Hennigsdorf.
Büssing	Büssing Automobilwerke, Braunschweig.
Charkov	Lokomotivwerk Charkov, Charkov, USSR.
Daimler-Benz	Daimler-Benz AG, Stuttgart.
Dessau	Dessauer Waggonfabrik, Dessau / VEB Waggonfabrik Dessau.
Deutz	Klöckner-Humboldt-Deutz AG, Köln.
Duewag	Düsseldorfer Waggonfabrik AG, Düsseldorf.
DWM	Deutsche Waggon- und Maschinenfabrik, Berlin.
Fuchs	H. Fuchs Waggonfabrik AG, Heidelberg.
Görlitz	VEB Waggonbau, Görlitz.
Gmeinder	Gmeinder & Co. GmbH, Mosbach.
Hannoversche	Hannoversche Maschinenbau AG, Hannover.
Henschel	Rheinstahl Henschel AG, Kassel (Now Thyssen Henschel AG).
Esslingen	Maschinenfabrik Esslingen, Esslingen.
IFA	VEB Ifa.
Johannisthal	VEB Motorenwerk, Johannisthal.
Jung	Arnold Jung Lokomotivfabrik GmbH, Jungenthal.
Kaeble	C. Kaeble Motorenfabrik, Backnang.
Kolomna	Lokomotivwerk Kolomna, Kolomna, USSR.
Krauss-Maffei	Krauss-Maffei AG, München.
Krupp	Friedrich Krupp Maschinenfabrik, Essen.
LEW	VEB Lokomotivbau und Elektrotechnische Werke, Hennigsdorf.
LHB	Link-Hoffman-Busch Waggon-Fahrzeug-Maschinen GmbH, Salzgitter.
LHW	Link-Hoffmann-Werke AG, Breslau (now in Poland).
LKM	VEB Lokomotivbau "Karl Marx", Babelsberg.
Lüttgens	Waggonfabrik Lüttgens GmbH, Saarbrücken.
MaK	Maschinenbau Kiel GmbH, Kiel.
MAN	Maschinenfabrik Augsburg-Nürnberg AG, Nürnberg.
Maybach	Maybach Motorenbau GmbH, Friedrichshafen.
MBB	Messerschmitt-Bölchow-Blohm GmbH, München.

Mercedes	Daimler-Benz AG, Stuttgart.
MTU	Motoren-und-Turbinen Union GmbH, Friedrichshafen.
MWM	Motoren-Werke Mannheim, Mannheim.
O & K	Orenstein-Koppel, Lübecker Maschinenbau AG, Dortmund.
Orion	Orion Werke, Eschwege.
Rathgeber	Waggonfabrik Josef Rathgeber AG, München.
Roßlau	VEB Elbewerk, Roßlau.
Schwartzkopff	Berliner Maschinenbau AG, Berlin.
Siemens	Siemens-Schuckert-Werk AG, Berlin & Erlangen.
Skoda	Skoda, Plzen, Czechoslovakia.
Strömungsmachinen	VEB Strömungsmaschinen, Pirna Sonnenstein.
Uerdingen	Waggonfabrik Uerdingen AG, Krefeld.
Voith	J.M. Voith GmbH, Heidenheim.
Voroshilovgrad	Voroshilovgrad Diesel Locomotive Works, Voroshilovgrad, USSR.
Vulcan	Schiffs und Maschinenbau Vulcan, Stettin.
Waggon Union	Waggon Union GmbH, Netphen.
Wegmann	Waggonfabrik Wegmann, Kassel.
Windhoff	Rheiner Maschinenfabrik Windhoff, Rheine.
Wismar	Triebwagen und Waggonfabrik Wismar, Wismar.
WMD	Waggon und Maschinenbau GmbH, Donauwörth.

Deutsche Bundesbahn (DB)

Gauge: 1435 mm; 1000 mm
Route Length: 27278 km (1435 mm); 4.6 km (1000 mm).

Depots

The DB network is divided into 10 divisions (Bundesbahndirektion - BD), each division having a number of depots (Bahnbetriebswerke - Bw). The codes shown below are those used within this publication, the first letter of each code denoting the appropriate division. The official codes are identical to the codes used in this book, except that suffix number 1 is added to all codes without a suffix number, with the exception of Köln, where the suffix number 2 is added. The suffix (Z) to a code indicates a vehicle currently stored.

BD HAMBURG

AFL	Flensburg		AK	Kiel
AH1	Hamburg Eidelstedt		AL	Lübeck
AH4	Hamburg Wilhelmsburg		AOP	Hamburg Ohlsdorf

BD ESSEN

EDO	Dortmund
EHG	Hagen
EHM	Hamm
EOB	Oberhausen (Osterfeld-Süd)
ESIE	Siegen
EWAN	Wanne-Eickel

BD FRANKFURT (MAIN)

FB	Bebra
FD	Darmstadt
FF1	Frankfurt (Main) 1
FF2	Frankfurt (Main) 2
FFU	Fulda
FG	Gießen
FK	Kassel
FL	Limburg/Lahn

BD HANNOVER

HA	Altenbeken
HB	Bremen
HBH	Bremerhaven
HE	Emden
HG	Göttingen
HH	Hannover
HO	Osnabrück
HOLD	Oldenburg
HS	Seelze
HWG	Wangerooge

BD KÖLN

KA	Aachen
KD	Düsseldorf
KG	Gremberg
KK	Köln Deutzerfeld
KKR	Krefeld
KM	Mönchengladbach
KW	Wuppertal

BD MÜNCHEN

MA	Augsburg
MFL	Freilassing
MH1	München Hbf
MH6	München Steinhausen
MIH	Ingolstadt
MKP	Kempten
MMF	Mühldorf

BD NÜRNBERG

NHO	Hof
NLF	Lichtenfels
NN1	Nürnberg Hbf
NN2	Nürnberg Rbf
NPA	Passau
NRH	Regensburg
NWH	Würzburg

BD KARLSRUHE

RF	Freiburg
RHL	Haltingen
RK	Karlsruhe
RM	Mannheim
RO	Offenburg
RSI	Singen

BD SAARBRÜCKEN

SKL	Kaiserslautern
SSH	Saarbrücken
STR	Trier

BD STUTTGART

TH	Heilbronn
TK	Stuttgart Kornwestheim
TP	Plochingen
TS	Stuttgart Hbf
TT	Tübingen
TU	Ulm

In addition, two workshops have locomotive allocations

HHX	Hannover-Leinhausen Works	KOPLX	Opladen Works

Workshops

The following DB owned workshops carry out overhaul and repair work to locomotives and multiple units:

Bremen-Sebaldsbrück
Classes 211, 212, 213, 214, 215, 216, 218, 290, 291, 323, 324, 331, 332, 333, 335.

Kassel
Classes 360, 361, 364, 365, 614, 624, 627, 628, 634, 796, 797, 798, 914, 924, 928, 934, 996, 997, 998.

München-Freimann
Classes 110, 111, 120, 139, 140, 150, 151, 420, 421, 491.

Nürnberg
Classes 217, 218, 290, 401, 403, 404, 410, 801, 810, 420, 421.

Opladen
Classes 103, 110, 111, 113, 114, 140, 141, 151, 181, 184.

In addition, some work for DB is carried out at the various DR workshops from time to time.

Deutsche Reichsbahn (DR)

Gauge: 1435 mm; 1000 mm; 900 mm; 750 mm; 600 mm.
Route **Length:** 13733 km (1435 mm); 274 km (various narrow gauges).

Depots

The DR network is divided into 5 divisions (Reichsbahndirektion - Rbd), each division having a number of depots (Bahnbetriebswerke - Bw). The codes shown are the unofficial codes used within this publication, based on the DB system of the first letter of each code denoting the appropriate division. (Z) in the allocation column denotes a vehicle which is currently stored. (ZR) denotes a vehicle currently held in reserve.

Rbd BERLIN

BB	Buchow	BF	Frankfurt (Oder)
BBF	Berlin-Friedrichsfelde	BG	Berlin-Grunewald
BBG	Berlin-Grünau	BH	Hoyerswerda
BBH	Berlin Hbf	BJ	Jüterbog
BBS	Berlin-Schöneweide	BP	Berlin-Pankow
BBW	Berlin-Wannsee	BSG	Senftenberg
BC	Cottbus	BSN	Seddin
BE	Elsterwerda	BW	Wustermark

Rbd DRESDEN

DA	Aue
DB	Bautzen
DC	Chemnitz
DD	Dresden
DGL	Glauchau
DGO	Görlitz
DK	Kamenz
DN	Nossen
DR	Reichenbach
DRI	Riesa
DZ	Zittau

Rbd ERFURT

UA	Arnstadt
UE	Eisenach
UER	Erfurt
UG	Gera
UM	Meiningen
UN	Nordhausen
UP	Probstzella
US	Saalfeld
USN	Sangerhausen
UW	Weißenfels

Rbd HALLE

LA	Altenburg
LB	Blankenburg
LBR	Brandenburg
LE	Engelsdorf
LF	Falkenburg
LG	Güsten
LH	Haldensleben

LHG	Halle G
LHP	Halle P
LHT	Halberstadt
LJ	Jerichow
LLS	Leipzig Hbf Süd
LLW	Leipzig Hbf West
LM	Magdeburg
LO	Oebisfelde
LR	Roßlau
LS	Salzwedel
LST	Stendal
LWA	Leipzig Wahren
LWE	Wernigerode
LWI	Wittenberg

Rbd SCHWERIN

CA	Angermünde
CE	Eberswalde
CG	Güstrow
CH	Heringsdorf
CHL	Hagenow Land
CM	Mukran
CN	Neubrandenburg
CNN	Neuruppin
CNZ	Neustrelitz
CP	Pasewalk
CR	Rostock
CRS	Rostock Seehafen
CS	Schwerin
CST	Stralsund
CWE	Wittenberge
CWI	Wismar

Workshops

The following DR owned workshops carry out overhaul and repair work to locomotives and multiple units:

Berlin Schöneweide
Classes 475, 476, 477, 478, 479, 485, 875, 876, 877, 878, 885.

Cottbus
Diesel Main Line Locomotives.

Dessau
Electric Locomotives.

Görlitz
Narrow Gauge Steam Locomotives.

Halle
Diesel Shunting Locomotives. Diesel Railcars.

Chemnitz
Diesel Main Line Locomotives.

Meiningen
Steam Locomotives.

Stendal
Diesel Main Line Locomotives.

Work is also carried out at the above under contract for the DB.

Railrover Information

German Rail Pass

5, 10 or 15 days unlimited travel (not necessarily consecutive) within a pre-designated one month period on all DB and DR trains (including all supplements except seat reservations, couchette or sleeper berths). The Pass is valid from 2300 on the day before to 0300 on the day after vaildity. For long overnight journeys this validity is extended to commence at 1900 on the day before validity. Also valid on long distance coach services operated within Germany by Deutsche Touring GmbH (DTG) and on daytime ship services of KD (Köln-Düsseldorfer Deutsche Rheinschiffahrt AG) between Köln and Mainz and between Koblenz and Cochem. Bus travel on DB operated local bus services is also available in many instances. A sheet of tear off vouchers is also provided with each Pass which gives discounts on a variety of other attractions, including Public Transport, Museums, Boat Trips, Rack and Cable Car services and Car Hire. A free "Thomas Cook Germany Timetable" (normally £2.50 is supplied with every Pass.

The Pass is available in three forms priced as follows (prices as at 01.02.92):

Single Pass (Adult fares. Children 4-11 pay 50% of these fares)
  5 Days - 1st Class £175.00; 2nd Class £115.00
10 Days - 1st Class £260.00; 2nd Class £175.00
15 Days - 1st Class £320.00; 2nd Class £215.00

Twin Pass (Any two adults travelling together)

5 Days - 1st Class £310.00; 2nd Class £205.00
10 Days - 1st Class £465.00; 2nd Class £310.00
15 Days - 1st Class £575.00; 2nd Class £385.00

Youth Pass (Young persons 12 to 25, 2nd Class only)

5 Days - £ 80.00
10 Days - £105.00
15 Days - £130.00

Regional Passes

5 or 10 days unlimited travel (not necessarily consecutive) within a pre-designated 21 day period on all DB and DR trains (including all supplements except on ICE services, seat reservations, couchette or sleeper berths) within the selected area. Regional Passes are not valid on bus services. Fifteen different area Passes are available as follows:

Region 101: Hamburg/Schleswig Holstein.
Region 102: Rostock/Schwerin/Baltic Coast.
Region 103: Bremen/Münster/North Sea Coast.
Region 104: Hanover/Lower Saxony.
Region 105: Hanover/Berlin/Harz.
Region 106: Berlin/Brandenburg.
Region 107: Köln/Düsseldorf/Rhine-Ruhr.
Region 108: Frankfurt/Hesse.
Region 109: Erfurt/Weimar/Thuringia.
Region 110: Dresden/Leipzig/Saxony.
Region 111: Köln/Mainz/Rhine-Moselle.
Region 112: Stuttgart/Neckar Schwabia/Black Forest/Lake Constance.
Region 113: Nürnberg/Franconia/Bavarian Forest.
Region 114: München/Bavarian Alps.
Region 115: Berlin/Dresden/Leipzig.

Regional Passes are available in three forms and are all the same price irrespective of area as follows (prices as at 01.02.92):

Single Pass (Adult fares)

5 Days - 1st Class £59.00; 2nd Class £39.00
10 Days - 1st Class £89.00; 2nd Class £59.00

Twin Pass (Any two adults travelling together)

5 Days - 1st Class £89.00; 2nd Class £59.00
10 Days - 1st Class £129.00; 2nd Class £89.00

Family Pass (One or two parents with any number of unmarried children under 18 years of age).

5 Days - 1st Class £99.00;   2nd Class £69.00
10 Days - 1st Class £149.00;   2nd Class £99.00

Special Notes
Proof of identity (i.e passport) is required at the time of purchase of any of the above tickets and must also be carried whilst travelling. During 1992 it is anticipated that some DR narrow gauge lines may be handed over to other operators. In this eventuality the validity of all the above passes may be affected - please enquire before travelling.

Tickets & Details
Further details and literature on all the above passes and rail travel in general in Germany is available from:

DER Travel Service,
German Rail Sales,
18 Conduit Street,
London,
W1R 9TD.
(Tel: 071-499-0577/78).

Other regional companies and also some BR Travel Centres also have available the above Passes for sale. A list of stockists is given in the publication "Travel Planner Germany", available from German Rail Distribution, 18 Chertsey Road, Woking, Surrey, GU21 5AB.

Timetable
The German railway timetable "Kursbuch" is widely available at railway stations, newsagents etc throughout Germany. Regional timetables are also available.
The Thomas Cook "Germany Timetable" may be purchased (price £3.00) from German Rail Distribution (see above for address).
Most main public libraries in the UK have the Kursbuch available in their reference section.

Tourist Information
Most major towns and cities in Germany have tourist offices at or near railway stations who are pleased to assist travellers in locating accommodation etc. These are of course more prevalent in the former West Germany than the East. Further information can be obtained in the UK from The German National Tourist Office, 61 Conduit Street, London, W1R 0EN. (Tel: 071-734-2600).

From experience it is fair to say that accommodation can usually be found at most locations on an ad hoc basis at reasonable prices provided that major festivals (i.e München Oktoberfest and "Messe" in various cities) are avoided.

Hotels used by readers of "European Report" are often listed in the magazine, together with details of service provided, cost, value for money etc.

Acknowledgements

The author is grateful to the following for their help in compiling this publication: Dale Fickes, Ronald Fischer, John Glossop, Phil Hodgson, Roger Morris, Philip Wormald, all the photographers who were kind enough to submit material and German Rail (London).

COVER PHOTOGRAPHS

Front Cover
Two of the magnificent DR 0-4-4-0 Mallets, 99 1564 & 99 1584 (new nos. 99 705 & 99 709 respectively), which provide power on the freight only Oschatz to Kemmlitz narrow gauge steam line, stand outside Mugeln depot during the lunchtime interval on 02.01.92, ready for their afternoon duties. (D.W. Fickes)

Back Cover
Berlin S-Bahn 275 363 arrives at Berlin Tiergarten 21.08.89 (R. Fischer)

STEAM LOCOMOTIVES

CLASS 041   2-8-2

Built: 1936-41.
Boiler Pressure: 20 kg/cm².
Cylinder Diameter: 2 x 520 mm.
Length Overall: 23.905 m. (Loco 15.100 m; Tender 8.805 m.)
Weight: 176.10 tonnes.
Wheel Diameters: 1000 + 1600 + 1250 mm.
Maximum Speed: 90 km/h.

041 025 (41 1025)	LG		041 150 (41 1150)	LG
041 137 (41 1137)	LG		041 231 (41 1231)	LG

CLASS 044   2-10-0

Built: 1926-44.
Boiler Pressure: 16 kg/cm².
Cylinder Diameter: 3 x 550 mm.
Length Overall: 22.620 m. (Loco 13.817m; Tender 8.803 m.)
Weight: 174.20 tonnes.
Wheel Diameter: 850 + 1400 mm.
Maximum Speed: 80 km/h.

044 105 (44 2105)	UE		044 412 (44 1412)	BC
044 106 (44 1106)	(Z)		044 486 (44 1486)	LG
044 115 (44 2115)	BH		044 537 (44 1537)	(Z)
044 167 (44 2167)	CG		044 546 (44 2546)	(Z)
044 182 (44 1182)	(Z)		044 593 (44 1593)	DC
044 196 (44 2196)	(Z)		044 600 (44 1600)	UER
044 251 (44 1251)	BC		044 614 (44 1614)	LE
044 351 (44 2351)	DC		044 661 (44 2661)	DB
044 378 (44 1378)	UER		044 687 (44 2687)	USN
044 397 (44 2397)	USN			

CLASS 050   2-10-0

Built: 1938-43.
Boiler Pressure: 16 kg/cm².
Cylinder Diameter: 600 mm.
Length Overall: 22.940 m. (Loco 13.680 m; Tender 9.260 m.)
Weight: 146.40 tonnes.
Wheel Diameter: 850 + 1400 mm.
Maximum Speed: 80 km/h.

▲ 41 1231 (new no. 041 231) + 44 1486 at Haldensleben on the 1540 Magdeburg - Oebisfelde 09.05.91 (D.J. Glossop).

▼ 44 1486 (new no. 044 486) near Haldensleben on the 1540 Magdeburg - Oebisfelde 10.05.91 (D.J. Glossop).

050 146 (50 2146)	(Z)	
050 506 (50 3506)	DD	
050 517 (50 3517)	(Z)	
050 518 (50 3518)	CA	
050 519 (50 3519)	DGL	
050 520 (50 3520)	LG	
050 521 (50 3521)	CP	
050 522 (50 3522)	CP	
050 523 (50 3523)	DR	
050 525 (50 3525)	(Z)	
050 527 (50 3527)	CNZ	
050 529 (50 3529)	DC	
050 535 (50 3535)	(Z)	
050 538 (50 3538)	(Z)	
050 539 (50 3539)	DN	
050 543 (50 3543)	(Z)	
050 545 (50 3545)	CWI	
050 551 (50 3551)	DC	
050 552 (50 3552)	LM	
050 553 (50 3553)	LG	
050 554 (50 3554)	DC	
050 555 (50 3555)	LE	
050 556 (50 3556)	(Z)	
050 557 (50 3557)	(Z)	
050 559 (50 3559)	(Z)	
050 562 (50 3562)	CNZ	
050 565 (50 3565)	DD	
050 570 (50 3570)	(Z)	
050 577 (50 3577)	(Z)	
050 581 (50 3581)	DC	
050 603 (50 3603)	DN	
050 604 (50 3604)	DC	
050 606 (50 3606)	LG	
050 610 (50 3610)	(Z)	
050 616 (50 3616)	DC	
050 618 (50 3618)	(Z)	
050 623 (50 3623)	(Z)	
050 624 (50 3624)	(Z)	
050 626 (50 3626)	LM	
050 628 (50 3628)	DC	
050 631 (50 3631)	(Z)	
050 635 (50 3635)	CA	
050 636 (50 3636)	DD	
050 638 (50 3638)	(Z)	
050 642 (50 3642)	(Z)	
050 645 (50 3645)	(Z)	
050 646 (50 3646)	DC	
050 648 (50 3648)	CE	
050 649 (50 3649)	LG	
050 652 (50 3652)	(Z)	
050 655 (50 3655)	DC	
050 657 (50 3657)	DD	
050 658 (50 3658)	DC	
050 661 (50 3661)	DD	
050 662 (50 3662)	(Z)	
050 666 (50 3666)	DC	
050 668 (50 3668)	(Z)	
050 670 (50 3670)	DR	
050 673 (50 3673)	DC	
050 680 (50 3680)	(Z)	
050 681 (50 3681)	(Z)	
050 682 (50 3682)	(Z)	
050 684 (50 3684)	(Z)	
050 685 (50 3685)	(Z)	
050 688 (50 3688)	DD	
050 689 (50 3689)	DR	
050 690 (50 3690)	DC	
050 691 (50 3691)	CWE	
050 693 (50 3693)	(Z)	
050 694 (50 3694)	(Z)	
050 695 (50 3695)	LG	
050 696 (50 3696)	DGL	
050 700 (50 3700)	LBR	
050 701 (50 3701)	(Z)	
050 704 (50 3704)	DC	
050 705 (50 3705)	LG	
050 707 (50 3707)	LM	
050 708 (50 3708)	LG	
052 001 (52 8001)	(Z)	
052 004 (52 8004)	BC	
052 006 (52 8006)	(Z)	
052 007 (52 8007)	(Z)	
052 008 (52 8008)	(Z)	
052 009 (52 8009)	DC	
052 010 (52 8010)	DZ	
052 012 (52 8012)	DZ	
052 013 (52 8013)	(Z)	
052 014 (52 8014)	(Z)	

▲ 52 8028 (new no. 052 028) on standby at Bw Engelsdorf 15.04.91　　　(D. Rowland)

▼ 99 5902 (new no. 099 111) at Drei Annen Hohne with the 0920 Wernigerode - Nordhausen Nord 28.07.90　　　　　　　　　　　　　　　(R.G. Morris)

052 015	(52 8015)	(Z)	052 090	(52 8090)	(Z)
052 017	(52 8017)	BF	052 091	(52 8091)	DGO
052 019	(52 8019)	(Z)	052 093	(52 8093)	(Z)
052 020	(52 8020)	DD	052 095	(52 8095)	BBS
052 021	(52 8021)	(Z)	052 096	(52 8096)	LA
052 023	(52 8023)	(Z)	052 097	(52 8097)	(Z)
052 027	(52 8027)	(Z)	052 098	(52 8098)	LHG
052 028	(52 8028)	(Z)	052 100	(52 8100)	(Z)
052 029	(52 8029)	BF	052 102	(52 8102)	(Z)
052 030	(52 8030)	CP	052 103	(52 8103)	(Z)
052 031	(52 8031)	(Z)	052 104	(52 8104)	(Z)
052 034	(52 8034)	LHG	052 105	(52 8105)	(Z)
052 035	(52 8035)	(Z)	052 106	(52 8106)	(Z)
052 036	(52 8036)	(Z)	052 108	(52 8108)	(Z)
052 037	(52 8037)	(Z)	052 109	(52 8109)	DB
052 038	(52 8038)	DZ	052 110	(52 8110)	(Z)
052 039	(52 8039)	LE	052 111	(52 8111)	(Z)
052 041	(52 8041)	LWI	052 113	(52 8113)	(Z)
052 042	(52 8042)	(Z)	052 114	(52 8114)	(Z)
052 043	(52 8043)	DN	052 115	(52 8115)	(Z)
052 046	(52 8046)	(Z)	052 116	(52 8116)	BC
052 047	(52 8047)	DZ	052 117	(52 8117)	BF
052 051	(52 8051)	DA	052 118	(52 8118)	BBS
052 055	(52 8055)	(Z)	052 119	(52 8119)	(Z)
052 057	(52 8057)	(Z)	052 120	(52 8120)	(Z)
052 058	(52 8058)	BH	052 121	(52 8121)	BC
052 062	(52 8062)	(Z)	052 122	(52 8122)	BC
052 063	(52 8063)	LF	052 123	(52 8123)	DB
052 064	(52 8064)	(Z)	052 124	(52 8124)	DK
052 068	(52 8068)	(Z)	052 125	(52 8125)	(Z)
052 069	(52 8069)	(Z)	052 126	(52 8126)	(Z)
052 072	(52 8072)	(Z)	052 129	(52 8129)	BBS
052 075	(52 8075)	BW	052 130	(52 8130)	(Z)
052 076	(52 8076)	(Z)	052 131	(52 8131)	(Z)
052 077	(52 8077)	(Z)	052 132	(52 8132)	(7)
052 078	(52 8078)	(Z)	052 133	(52 8133)	(Z)
052 079	(52 8079)	BBS	052 134	(52 8134)	BE
052 080	(52 8080)	(Z)	052 137	(52 8137)	(Z)
052 082	(52 8082)	(Z)	052 138	(52 8138)	(Z)
052 083	(52 8083)	(Z)	052 139	(52 8139)	(Z)
052 085	(52 8085)	(Z)	052 141	(52 8141)	CA
052 086	(52 8086)	(Z)	052 142	(52 8142)	(Z)
052 087	(52 8087)	BBS	052 143	(52 8143)	(Z)
052 089	(52 8089)	(Z)	052 145	(52 8145)	BF

052 147 (52 8147)	(Z)	052 180 (52 8180)	(Z)
052 148 (52 8148)	BC	052 183 (52 8183)	(Z)
052 149 (52 8149)	DC	052 184 (52 8184)	LBR
052 152 (52 8152)	(Z)	052 185 (52 8185)	(Z)
052 154 (52 8154)	LHG	052 186 (52 8186)	(Z)
052 156 (52 8156)	LBR	052 187 (52 8187)	(Z)
052 157 (52 8157)	(Z)	052 189 (52 8189)	(Z)
052 160 (52 8160)	DZ	052 190 (52 8190)	BC
052 161 (52 8161)	(Z)	052 191 (52 8191)	(Z)
052 163 (52 8163)	BC	052 194 (52 8194)	(Z)
052 168 (52 8168)	LE	052 195 (52 2195)	(Z)
052 169 (52 8169)	(Z)	052 195 (52 8195)	DZ
052 170 (52 8170)	BBS	052 196 (52 8196)	(Z)
052 171 (52 8171)	LBR	052 197 (52 8197)	(Z)
052 173 (52 8173)	LHT	052 198 (52 8198)	(Z)
052 174 (52 8174)	LF	052 199 (52 8199)	(Z)
052 175 (52 8175)	(Z)	052 200 (52 8200)	DB
052 176 (52 8176)	DN	052 662 (52 1662)	(Z)
052 177 (52 8177)	(Z)	052 721 (52 6721)	(Z)

CLASS 058   2-10-0

Built: 1920 by Borsig - Rebuilt 1958-63 by DR Zwickau works.
Boiler Pressure: 16 kg/cm²
Cylinder Diameter: 3 x 570 mm.
Length Overall: 22.110 m.
Weight: 125.2 tonnes.
Wheel Diameter: 1000 + 1400 mm.
Maximum Speed: 70 km/h.

058 049 (58 3049) DGL

CLASS 065   2-8-4T

Built: 1957 by LKM.
Boiler Pressure: 16 kg/cm².
Cylinder Diameter: 2 x 600 mm.
Length: 17.500 m.
Weight: 121.7 tonnes.
Wheel Diameter: 1000 + 1600 + 1000 mm.
Maximum Speed: 90 km/h.

065 008 (65 1008) BC

CLASS 086

2-8-2T

Built: 1928-42.
Boiler Pressure: 14 kg/cm².
Length: 13.820 or 13.920 m.
Wheel Diameter: 850 + 1400 + 850 mm.

Cylinder Diameter: 2 x 570 mm.
Weight: 88.5 or 87.3 tonnes.
Maximum Speed: 80 km/h.

086 049 (86 1049)   DC
086 333 (86 1333)   DC

086 501 (86 1501)   (Z)

CLASS 095

2-10-2T

Built: 1922 onwards by Borsig
Boiler Pressure: 14 kg/cm².
Length: 15.100 m.
Wheel Diameter: 850 + 1400 + 850 mm.

Cylinder Diameter: 2 x 700 mm.
Weight: 127.4 tonnes.
Maximum Speed: 70 km/h.

095 016 (95 1016)   (Z)

NARROW GAUGE STEAM LOCOMOTIVES

099 110-112

0-4-4-0T

Gauge: 1000 mm.
Built: 1899 by Jung.
Boiler Pressure: 14 kg/cm².
Length: 8.874 m.
Wheel Diameter: 1000 + 1000 mm.

Cylinder Diameter: 285/425 mm.
Weight: 36.00 tonnes.
Maximum Speed: 30 km/h.

099 110 (99 5901)   (Z)
099 111 (99 5902)   LWE

099 112 (99 5903) LWE

099 113

0-4-4-0T

Gauge: 1000 mm.
Built: 1918 by Jung.
Boiler Pressure: 12 kg/cm².
Length: 9.400 m.
Wheel Diameter: 1000 + 1000 mm.

Cylinder Diameter: 280/425 mm.
Weight: 36.00 tonnes.
Maximum Speed: 30 km/h.

099 113 (99 5906)   LWE

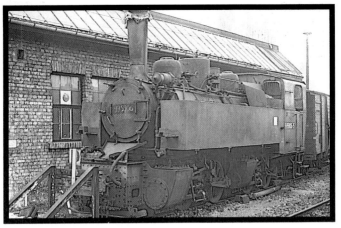

▲ 99 5906 (new no. 099 113) at Wernigerode-Westerntor Works Yard 26.03.91
(B.A. Hawkins)

▼ 99 6001 (new no. 099 120) at Drei Annen Hohne 28.07.90   (R.G. Morris)

099 120   2-6-2T

Gauge: 1000 mm.
Built: 1939 by Krupp.
Boiler Pressure: 14 kg/cm².   **Cylinder Diameter:** 420 mm.
Length: 8.910 m.   **Weight:** 47.60 tonnes.
Wheel Diameters: 600 + 1000 + 600 mm.   **Maximum Speed:** 50 km/h.

099 120 (99 6001)   LWE

099 130   0-6-0T

Gauge: 1000 mm.
Built: 1914 by Henschel.
Boiler Pressure: 14 kg/cm².   **Cylinder Diameter:** 400 mm.
Length: 7.734 m.   **Weight:** 32.00 tonnes.
Wheel Diameter: 800 mm.   **Maximum Speed:** 30 km/h.

099 130 (99 6101)   LWE

099 140   2-10-2T

Gauge: 1000 mm.
Built: 1931 by Schwartzkopff.
Boiler Pressure: 14 kg/cm².   **Cylinder Diameter:** 550 mm.
Length: 11.636 m.   **Weight:** 65.80 tonnes.
Wheel Diameters: 550 + 1000 + 550 mm.   **Maximum Speed:** 40 km/h.

099 140 (99 7222)   LWE

099 141-157   2-10-2T

Gauge: 1000 mm.
Built: 1954-57 by LKM.
Boiler Pressure: 14 kg/cm².   **Cylinder Diameter:** 500 mm.
Length: 11.730 m.   **Weight:** 64.50 tonnes.
Wheel Diameters: 550 + 1000 + 550 mm.   **Maximum Speed:** 40 km/h.

099 141 (99 7231)	LWE	099 146 (99 7236)	LWE
099 142 (99 7232)	LWE	099 147 (99 7237)	LWE
099 143 (99 7233)	LWE	099 148 (99 7238)	LWE
099 144 (99 7234)	LWE	099 149 (99 7239)	LWE
099 145 (99 7235)	LWE	099 150 (99 7240)	LWE

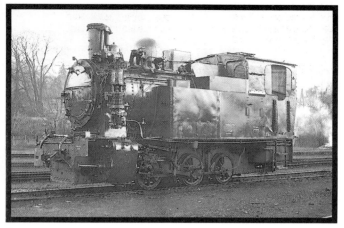

▲ 99 6101 (new no. 099 130) at Gernrode 28.03.91   (B.A. Hawkins)

▼ 99 7246 (new no. 099 156) at Nordhausen with the mid morning train to Hasselfelde
11.09.90   (D.W. Fickes).

099 151 (99 7241)	LWE		099 155 (99 7245)	LWE
099 152 (99 7242)	LWE		099 156 (99 7246)	LWE
099 153 (99 7243)	LWE		099 157 (99 7247)	LWE
099 154 (99 7244)	LWE			

099 701-713   0-4-4-0T

Gauge: 750 mm.
Built: 1899-1922 by Hartmann. Rebuilt 1962 by DR.
Boiler Pressure: 15 kg/cm².   **Cylinder Diameter:** 240/370/400 mm.
Length: 9.000 m.   **Weight:** 26.80-29.30 tonnes.
Wheel Diameter: 750 + 750 mm.   **Maximum Speed:** 30 km/h.

099 701 (99 1539)	DN		099 708 (99 1582)	DN
099 702 (99 1542)	DN		099 709 (99 1584)	DN
099 703 (99 1561)	DN		099 710 (99 1585)	DN
099 704 (99 1562)	(Z)		099 711 (99 1586)	DA
099 705 (99 1564)	DN		099 712 (99 1606)	DN
099 706 (99 1568)	DN		099 713 (99 1608)	DN
099 707 (99 1574)	DN			

099 720-721   0-10-0T

Gauge: 750 mm.
Built: 1927 by Hartmann.
Boiler Pressure: **Cylinder Diameter:**
Length: **Weight:**
Wheel Diameter: **Maximum Speed:**

099 720 (99 1713)	DN	099 721 (99 1715)	(Z)

099 722-735   2-10-2T

Gauge: 750 mm.
Built: 1928-33 by Hartmann/Schwartzkopff.
Boiler Pressure: 14 kg/cm².
Cylinder Diameter: 450 mm.
Length: 10.450 m.
Weight: 56.70 tonnes.
Wheel Diameters: 550 + 800 + 550 mm.
Maximum Speed: 30 km/h.

099 722 (99 1731)	DZ	099 725 (99 1741)	DZ
099 723 (99 1734)	DN	099 726 (99 1746)	DN
099 724 (99 1735)	DZ	099 727 (99 1747)	DZ

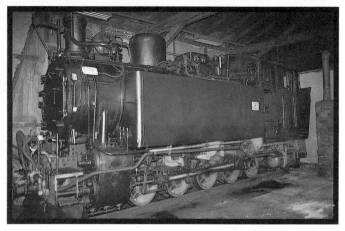

▲ 99 713 (new no. 099 720) inside the depot at Radebeul Ost 30.07.90   (R.G. Morris)

▼ 99 1749 (new no. 099 728) stands at Zittau ready to depart for Kurort Jonsdorf 15.09.90
(D.W. Fickes)

099 728 (99 1749)	DZ		099 732 (99 1759)	DZ
099 729 (99 1750)	DZ		099 733 (99 1760)	DZ
099 730 (99 1757)	DZ		099 734 (99 1761)	DN
099 731 (99 1758)	DZ		099 735 (99 1762)	DN

099 736-757   2-10-2T

Gauge: 750 mm.
Built: 1952-56 by LKM.
Boiler Pressure: 14 kg/cm².
Cylinder Diameter: 450 mm.
Length: 11.300 m.
Weight: 55.00 tonnes.
Wheel Diameters: 550 + 800 + 550 mm.
Maximum Speed: 30 km/h.

099 736 (99 1771)	DA		099 747 (99 1783)	DN
099 737 (99 1772)	DA		099 748 (99 1784)	CST
099 738 (99 1773)	DA		099 749 (99 1785)	DA
099 739 (99 1775)	DN		099 750 (99 1786)	DA
099 740 (99 1776)	DA		099 751 (99 1787)	DN
099 741 (99 1777)	DN		099 752 (99 1788)	DA
099 742 (99 1778)	DN		099 753 (99 1789)	DN
099 743 (99 1779)	DN		099 754 (99 1790)	DN
099 744 (99 1780)	DN		099 755 (99 1791)	DA
099 745 (99 1781)	DN		099 756 (99 1793)	DN
099 746 (99 1782)	CST		099 757 (99 1794)	DN

099 760   0-8-0T

Gauge: 750 mm.
Built: 1924 by O & K.
Boiler Pressure: 12 kg/cm².   **Cylinder Diameter:** 300 mm.
Length: 6.930 m.   **Weight:** 41.00 tonnes.
Wheel Diameter: 750 mm.   **Maximum Speed:** 25 km/h.

099 760 (99 4532)   (Z)

099 770-771   0-8-0T

Gauge: 750 mm.
Built: 1914/25 by Vulcan.
Boiler Pressure: 12 kg/cm².   **Cylinder Diameter:** 350 mm.

▲ 99 1758 (new no. 099 731) stands spare at Bw Zittau 15.09.90 (D.W. Fickes)

▼ 99 2322 (new no. 099 902) at Ostseebad Kühlungsborn West 05.04.91 (T. Rogers)

Length: 8.000 m.
Wheel Diameter: 850 mm.

Weight: 24.00 tonnes.
Maximum Speed: 30 km/h.

099 770 (99 4632)   CST

099 771 (99 4633)   (Z)

099 780-781   0-8-0T

Gauge: 750 mm.
Built: 1938 by Henschel.
Boiler Pressure: 13 kg/cm².
Length: 9.440 m.
Wheel Diameter: 850 mm.

Cylinder Diameter: 360 mm.
Weight: 32.40 tonnes.
Maximum Speed: 40 km/h.

099 780 (99 4801)   CST

099 781 (99 4802)   CST

099 901-903   2-8-2T

Gauge: 900 mm.
Built: 1932 by O & K.
Boiler Pressure: 14 kg/cm².
Length: 10.595 m.
Wheel Diameters: 550 + 1100 + 550 mm

Cylinder Diameter: 380 mm.
Weight: 43.68 tonnes.
Maximum Speed: 50 km/h.

099 901 (99 2321)   CR
099 902 (99 2322)   CR

099 903 (99 2323)   CR

099 904-905   0-8-0T

Gauge: 900 mm.
Built: 1950-51 by LKM.
Boiler Pressure: 14 kg/cm².
Length: 8.860 m.
Wheel Diameter: 800 mm.

Cylinder Diameter: 370 mm.
Weight: 32.40 tonnes.
Maximum Speed: 35 km/h.

099 904 (99 2331)   CR

099 905 (99 2332)   CR

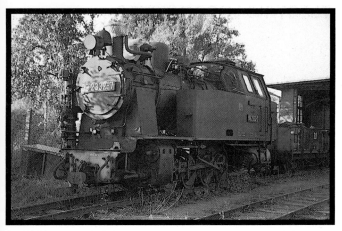

▲ 99 2332 (new no. 099 905) at Ostseebad Kühlungsborn 28.10.91   (R.G. Morris)

▼ 99 4801 (new no. 099 780) at Gohren 28.10.90   (R.G. Morris)

ELECTRIC LOCOMOTIVES

CLASS 103   Co-Co

Built: 1970-74 by Henschel/Krauss-Maffei/Krupp.
System: 15 kV ac 16.67 Hz ac overhead.
Electrical Equipment: Siemens/AEG/BBC.
Continuous Rating: 7440 kW.
Weight: 114 tonnes.
Length: 19.500 m. (* 20.200 m.)
Maximum Speed: 200 km/h.
Train Heating: Electric (1000 V system).

103 101 FF1	103 133 FF1	103 163 FF1
103 102 FF1	103 134 FF1	103 164 FF1
103 103 FF1	103 135 FF1(Z)	103 165 FF1
103 104 FF1	103 136 FF1	103 166 FF1
103 105 FF1	103 137 FF1	103 167 FF1
103 107 FF1	103 138 FF1	103 168 FF1
103 108 FF1	103 139 FF1	103 169 FF1
103 109 FF1	103 140 FF1	103 170 FF1
103 110 FF1	103 141 FF1	103 171 FF1
103 111 FF1	103 142 FF1	103 172 FF1
103 112 FF1	103 143 FF1	103 173* AH1
103 113 FF1	103 144 FF1	103 174 AH1
103 114 FF1	103 145 FF1	103 175 AH1
103 115 FF1	103 146 FF1	103 176 FF1
103 116 FF1	103 147 FF1	103 177 AH1
103 117 FF1	103 148 FF1	103 178 AH1
103 118 FF1	103 149 FF1	103 179 AH1
103 119 FF1	103 150 FF1	103 180 AH1
103 120 FF1	103 151 FF1	103 181 AH1
103 121 FF1	103 152 FF1	103 182 AH1
103 122 FF1	103 153 FF1	103 183 AH1
103 123 FF1	103 154 FF1	103 184 AH1
103 124 FF1	103 155 FF1	103 185 AH1
103 126 FF1	103 156 FF1	103 186 AH1
103 127 FF1	103 157 FF1	103 187 AH1
103 128 FF1	103 158 FF1	103 188 AH1
103 129 FF1	103 159 FF1	103 189 AH1
103 130 FF1	103 160 FF1	103 190 AH1
103 131 FF1	103 161 FF1	103 191 AH1
103 132 FF1	103 162 FF1	103 192 AH1

▲ 103 172 at Ludwigsburg with D2199 Hamburg Altona - Stuttgart 24.02.90 (R. Fischer)

▼ 211 094 (new number 109 094) at Bw Leipzig West 01.01.92   (D.W. Fickes)

103 193 AH1	103 211 AH1	103 230* AH1
103 194 AH1	103 212 AH1	103 231* AH1
103 195 AH1	103 213 AH1	103 232* AH1
103 196 AH1	103 214 AH1	103 233* AH1
103 197 AH1	103 215 AH1	103 234* AH1
103 198 AH1	103 216* AH1	103 235* AH1
103 199 AH1	103 217* AH1	103 236* AH1
103 200 AH1	103 218* AH1	103 237* AH1
103 201 AH1	103 219* AH1	103 238* AH1
103 202 AH1	103 220* AH1	103 239* AH1
103 203 AH1	103 221* AH1	103 240* AH1
103 204 AH1	103 223* AH1	103 241* AH1
103 205 AH1	103 224* AH1	103 242* AH1
103 206 AH1	103 225* AH1	103 243* AH1
103 207 AH1	103 226* AH1	103 244* AH1
103 208 AH1	103 227* AH1	103 245* AH1
103 209 AH1	103 228* AH1	
103 210 AH1	103 229* AH1	

CLASS 109   Bo-Bo

Built: 1961-76 by LEW.
System: 15 kV 16.67 Hz overhead.
Electrical Equipment: LEW.
Continuous Rating: 2740 kW.
Weight: 82.5 tonnes.
Length: 16.260 m.
Maximum Speed: 120 km/h.
Train Heating: Electric (1000 V system).
Notes: All equipped for push-pull working.

Class 109.0 Standard Design.

109 001 (211 001)	LHP	109 022 (211 022)	LLW
109 002 (211 002)	LHP	109 023 (211 023)	LLW
109 003 (211 003)	LHP	109 024 (211 024)	LHP
109 007 (211 007)	BBS	109 025 (211 025)	LLW
109 009 (211 009)	BBS	109 028 (211 028)	LLW
109 013 (211 013)	LLW	109 029 (211 029)	LLW
109 014 (211 014)	BBS	109 034 (211 034)	LLW
109 015 (211 015)	BBS	109 036 (211 036)	BBS
109 017 (211 017)	BBS	109 042 (211 042)	LLW
109 018 (211 018)	BBS	109 043 (211 043)	CNZ
109 019 (211 019)	BBS	109 044 (211 044)	LLW
109 020 (211 020)	LLW	109 045 (211 045)	BBS
109 021 (211 021)	BBS	109 047 (211 047)	LLW

109 048 (211 048)	CST	109 073 (211 073)	BBS
109 049 (211 049)	CST	109 075 (211 075)	BBS
109 050 (211 050)	CNZ	109 079 (211 079)	CST
109 052 (211 052)	LLW	109 080 (211 080)	LHP
109 053 (211 053)	BBS	109 082 (211 082)	CNZ
109 057 (211 057)	LM	109 084 (211 084)	CNZ
109 058 (211 058)	LLW	109 085 (211 085)	(Z)
109 059 (211 059)	LLW	109 086 (211 086)	(Z)
109 060 (211 060)	LLW	109 088 (211 088)	CNZ
109 061 (211 061)	CNZ	109 089 (211 089)	BBS
109 062 (211 062)	CST	109 090 (211 090)	LHP
109 067 (211 067)	LLW	109 091 (211 091)	LHP
109 069 (211 069)	LHP	109 092 (211 092)	LM
109 070 (211 070)	BBS	109 094 (211 094)	LHP
109 071 (211 071)	BBS	109 096 (211 096)	LHP
109 072 (211 072)	BBS		

CLASS 109.8. Equipped for multiple working.

109 808 (211 808)	LM	109 833 (211 833)	LM
109 811 (211 811)	LM	109 835 (211 835)	LM
109 812 (211 812)	LM	109 839 (211 839)	LM

CLASS 110   Bo-Bo

Built: 1956-69 by Henschel/Krauss-Maffei/Krupp.
System: 15 kV ac 16.67 Hz ac overhead.
Electrical Equipment: BBC/Siemens/AEG.
Continuous Rating: 3620 kW.
Weight: 84.6 tonnes.
Length: 16.490 m.
Maximum Speed: 150 km/h
Train Heating: Electric (1000 V system).
Notes: 110 511 was converted from 139 134 in 1985. 110 494 was converted from 114 494 in 1991.

CLASS 110.1 Original Body Design (110 107/271 were rebuilt to later design after collision damage).

110 102 FF1	110 110 FF1	110 117 KK
110 103 FF1	110 111 FF1	110 118 KK
110 105 FF1	110 112 FF1	110 119 KK
110 106 FF1	110 113 FF1	110 120 KK
110 107 FF1	110 114 FF1	110 121 KK
110 108 FF1	110 115 FF1	110 122 KK
110 109 FF1	110 116 FF1	110 123 KK

110 124 KK	110 168 FF1	110 212 FF1
110 125 KK	110 169 TS	110 213 FF1
110 126 KK	110 170 TS	110 214 FF1
110 127 KK	110 171 TS	110 215 FF1
110 128 KK	110 172 TS	110 216 TS
110 129 KK	110 173 TS	110 217 TS
110 130 KK	110 174 TS	110 218 TS
110 131 KK	110 175 TS	110 219 TS
110 132 KK	110 176 TS	110 220 TS
110 133 KK	110 177 TS	110 221 TS
110 134 KK	110 178 TS	110 222 TS
110 135 KK	110 179 TS	110 223 TS
110 136 KK	110 180 TS	110 224 TS
110 137 KK	110 181 TS	110 225 TS
110 138 KK	110 182 TS	110 226 TS
110 139 KK	110 183 TS	110 227 TS
110 140 KK	110 184 TS	110 228 TS
110 141 KK	110 185 TS	110 229 TS
110 142 KK	110 186 TS	110 230 TS
110 143 KK	110 187 TS	110 231 TS
110 144 KK	110 188 TS	110 232 TS
110 145 KK	110 189 TS	110 233 TS
110 146 KK	110 190 TS	110 234 TS
110 147 KK	110 191 TS	110 235 TS
110 148 KK	110 192 TS	110 236 TS
110 149 KK	110 193 TS	110 237 TS
110 150 KK	110 194 TS	110 238 TS
110 151 KK	110 195 TS	110 239 TS
110 152 KK	110 196 TS	110 240 TS
110 153 KK	110 197 TS	110 241 EDO
110 154 FF1	110 198 TS	110 242 EDO
110 155 KK	110 199 KK	110 243 EDO
110 156 KK	110 200 KK	110 244 EDO
110 157 KK	110 201 EDO	110 245 EDO
110 158 KK	110 202 EDO	110 246 EDO
110 159 KK	110 203 EDO	110 247 EDO
110 160 KK	110 204 EDO	110 248 EDO
110 161 KK	110 205 EDO	110 249 EDO
110 162 FF1	110 206 EDO	110 250 EDO
110 163 FF1	110 207 EDO	110 251 EDO
110 164 FF1	110 208 EDO	110 252 EDO
110 165 FF1	110 209 EDO	110 253 EDO
110 166 TS	110 210 FF1	110 254 EDO
110 167 TS	110 211 FF1	110 255 EDO

▲ 110 126 at Oberhausen with the 1249 Amsterdam - Köln 14.08.90   (J. Hayes)

▼ 110 206 at Bw Altenbeken 24.02.90   (R.G. Morris)

110 256 KK	110 271 FF1	110 280 KK
110 257 KK	110 272 KK	110 281 KK
110 258 KK	110 273 KK	110 282 KK
110 259 KK	110 274 KK	110 283 KK
110 260 KK	110 275 KK	110 284 AH1
110 261 KK	110 276 KK	110 285 AH1
110 262 KK	110 277 KK	110 286 AH1
110 263 KK	110 278 KK	110 287 AH1
110 264 KK	110 279 KK	

CLASS 110.3 Revised Body Design.

110 288 FF1	110 326 KK	110 359 AH1
110 289 FF1	110 327 AH1	110 360 AH1
110 290 TS	110 328 AH1	110 361 AH1
110 291 TS	110 329 AH1	110 362 AH1
110 292 AH1	110 330 AH1	110 363 AH1
110 293 TS	110 331 AH1	110 364 AH1
110 294 TS	110 332 FF1	110 365 AH1
110 295 TS	110 333 FF1	110 366 AH1
110 296 TS	110 334 FF1	110 367 AH1
110 297 TS	110 335 FF1	110 368 AH1
110 298 AH1	110 336 FF1	110 369 AH1
110 299 AH1	110 337 FF1	110 370 AH1
110 300 AH1	110 338 FF1	110 371 AH1
110 301 AH1	110 339 FF1	110 372 AH1
110 302 AH1	110 340 FF1	110 373 AH1
110 303 AH1	110 341 FF1	110 374 AH1
110 304 KK	110 342 FF1	110 375 AH1
110 305 KK	110 343 FF1	110 376 AH1
110 306 KK	110 344 KK	110 377 AH1
110 307 KK	110 345 FF1	110 378 AH1
110 313 KK	110 346 FF1	110 379 AH1
110 314 KK	110 347 FF1	110 380 AH1
110 315 KK	110 348 FF1	110 381 AH1
110 316 KK	110 349 FF1	110 382 AH1
110 317 KK	110 350 FF1	110 383 AH1
110 318 KK	110 351 FF1	110 384 AH1
110 319 KK	110 352 KK	110 386 FF1
110 320 KK	110 353 KK	110 387 FF1
110 321 AH1	110 354 KK	110 388 FF1
110 322 AH1	110 355 KK	110 389 FF1
110 323 AH1	110 356 KK	110 390 FF1
110 324 KK	110 357 KK	110 391 FF1
110 325 KK	110 358 AH1	110 392 FF1

110 393 EDO	110 426 EDO	110 460 EDO
110 394 EDO	110 427 EDO	110 461 EDO
110 395 EDO	110 428 EDO	110 462 EDO
110 396 EDO	110 429 EDO	110 463 EDO
110 397 EDO	110 430 EDO	110 464 EDO
110 398 EDO	110 431 EDO	110 465 EDO
110 399 EDO	110 432 EDO	110 466 EDO
110 400 EDO	110 434 EDO	110 467 EDO
110 401 EDO	110 435 EDO	110 468 EDO
110 402 EDO	110 436 EDO	110 469 EDO
110 403 EDO	110 437 EDO	110 470 EDO
110 404 EDO	110 438 EDO	110 471 EDO
110 405 EDO	110 439 EDO	110 472 EDO
110 406 EDO	110 440 EDO	110 473 EDO
110 407 EDO	110 441 EDO	110 474 EDO
110 408 EDO	110 442 EDO	110 475 EDO
110 409 EDO	110 443 EDO	110 476 EDO
110 410 EDO	110 444 EDO	110 478 EDO
110 411 EDO	110 445 EDO	110 479 EDO
110 412 EDO	110 446 EDO	110 480 EDO
110 413 EDO	110 447 EDO	110 481 EDO
110 414 EDO	110 448 EDO	110 482 EDO
110 415 EDO	110 449 EDO	110 483 EDO
110 416 EDO	110 450 EDO	110 484 EDO
110 417 EDO	110 451 EDO	110 494 AH1
110 418 EDO	110 452 EDO	110 505 EDO
110 419 EDO	110 453 EDO	110 506 EDO
110 420 EDO	110 454 EDO	110 507 EDO
110 421 EDO	110 455 EDO	110 508 EDO
110 422 EDO	110 456 EDO	110 509 EDO
110 423 EDO	110 457 EDO	110 510 EDO
110 424 EDO	110 458 EDO	
110 425 EDO	110 459 EDO	

CLASS 110.1 Original Body Design.
110 511 EDO

CLASS 111   Bo-Bo

Built: 1975-84 by Henschel/Krauss-Maffei/Krupp.
System: 15 kV ac 16.67 Hz ac overhead.
Electrical Equipment: BBC/Siemens/AEG.
Continuous Rating: 3850 kW.
Weight: 83.0 tonnes.
Length: 16.750 m.

Maximum Speed: 160 km/h.
Train Heating: Electric (1000 V system).
Notes: All equipped for multiple working/push-pull working.

111 001 MH1	111 042 MH1	111 083 MH1
111 002 MH1	111 043 MH1	111 084 MH1
111 003 MH1	111 044 MH1	111 085 MH1
111 004 MH1	111 045 MH1	111 086 MH1
111 005 MH1	111 046 MH1	111 087 MH1
111 006 MH1	111 047 MH1	111 088 FF1
111 007 MH1	111 048 MH1	111 089 FF1
111 008 MH1	111 049 FF1	111 090 FF1
111 009 MH1	111 050 MH1	111 091 FF1
111 010 MH1	111 051 MH1	111 092 FF1
111 011 MH1	111 052 MH1	111 093 FF1
111 012 MH1	111 053 MH1	111 094 FF1
111 013 MH1	111 054 MH1	111 095 FF1
111 014 MH1	111 055 MH1	111 096 FF1
111 015 MH1	111 056 MH1	111 097 FF1
111 016 MH1	111 057 MH1	111 098 FF1
111 017 MH1	111 058 MH1	111 099 FF1
111 018 MH1	111 059 MH1	111 100 FF1
111 019 MH1	111 060 MH1	111 101 FF1
111 020 MH1	111 061 MH1	111 102 FF1
111 021 MH1	111 062 MH1	111 103 FF1
111 022 MH1	111 063 MH1	111 104 FF1
111 023 MH1	111 064 MH1	111 105 FF1
111 024 MH1	111 065 MH1	111 106 FF1
111 025 MH1	111 066 MH1	111 107 FF1
111 026 MH1	111 067 MH1	111 108 FF1
111 027 MH1	111 068 MH1	111 110 FF1
111 028 MH1	111 069 MH1	111 111 KD
111 029 MH1	111 070 MH1	111 112 KD
111 030 MH1	111 071 MH1	111 113 KD
111 031 MH1	111 072 MH1	111 114 KD
111 032 MH1	111 073 MH1	111 115 KD
111 033 MH1	111 074 MH1	111 116 KD
111 034 MH1	111 075 MH1	111 117 KD
111 035 MH1	111 076 MH1	111 118 KD
111 036 MH1	111 077 MH1	111 119 KD
111 037 MH1	111 078 MH1	111 120 KD
111 038 MH1	111 079 MH1	111 121 KD
111 039 MH1	111 080 MH1	111 122 KD
111 040 MH1	111 081 MH1	111 123 KD
111 041 MH1	111 082 MH1	111 124 KD

▲ 111 182 at Bergisch Gladbach on the rear of the 1357 S-Bahn train to Köln Worringen
(J. Hayes)

▼ Recently delivered 112 011 at Bw Leipzig West 01.01.92   (D.W. Fickes)

111 125 KD	111 160 KD	111 195 MH1
111 126 KD	111 161 KD	111 196 MH1
111 127 KD	111 162 KD	111 197 MH1
111 128 KD	111 163 KD	111 198 MH1
111 129 KD	111 164 KD	111 199 MH1
111 130 KD	111 165 KD	111 200 MH1
111 131 KD	111 166 KD	111 201 MH1
111 132 KD	111 167 KD	111 202 MH1
111 133 KD	111 168 KD	111 203 MH1
111 134 KD	111 169 KD	111 204 MH1
111 135 KD	111 170 KD	111 205 MH1
111 136 KD	111 171 KD	111 206 MH1
111 137 KD	111 172 KD	111 207 MH1
111 138 KD	111 173 KD	111 208 MH1
111 139 KD	111 174 KD	111 209 MH1
111 140 KD	111 175 KD	111 210 MH1
111 141 KD	111 176 KD	111 211 MH1
111 142 KD	111 177 KD	111 212 MH1
111 143 KD	111 178 KD	111 213 MH1
111 144 KD	111 179 KD	111 214 MH1
111 145 KD	111 180 KD	111 215 MH1
111 146 KD	111 181 KD	111 216 MH1
111 147 KD	111 182 KD	111 217 MH1
111 148 KD	111 183 KD	111 218 MH1
111 149 KD	111 184 KD	111 219 MH1
111 150 KD	111 185 KD	111 220 MH1
111 151 KD	111 186 KD	111 221 MH1
111 152 KD	111 187 KD	111 222 MH1
111 153 KD	111 188 KD	111 223 MH1
111 154 KD	111 189 MH1	111 224 MH1
111 155 KD	111 190 MH1	111 225 MH1
111 156 KD	111 191 MH1	111 226 MH1
111 157 KD	111 192 MH1	111 227 MH1
111 158 KD	111 193 MH1	
111 159 KD	111 194 MH1	

CLASS 112   Bo-Bo

Built: 1990 onwards by LEW.
System: 15 kV 16.67 Hz overhead.
Electrical Equipment: LEW.
Continuous Rating: 3500 kW.
Weight: 82.5 tonnes.
Length: 16.640 m.
Maximum Speed: 140 km/h.
Train Heating: Electric (1000 V system).

112 002 (212 002)	BBH	112 040
112 003 (212 003)	BBH	112 041
112 004 (212 004)	BBH	112 042
112 005 (212 005)	BBH	112 043
112 006	BBH	112 044
112 007	BBH	112 045
112 008	BBH	112 046
112 009	BBH	112 047
112 010	BBH	112 048
112 011	BBH	112 049
112 012	BBH	112 050
112 013	BBH	112 051
112 014	BBH	112 052
112 015	BBH	112 053
112 016	BBH	112 054
112 017	BBH	112 055
112 018	BBH	112 056
112 019	BBH	112 057
112 020	BBH	112 058
112 021	BBH	112 059
112 022	BBH	112 060
112 023	BBH	112 061
112 024	BBH	112 062
112 025	BBH	112 063
112 026	BBH	112 064
112 027	BBH	112 065
112 028	BBH	112 066
112 029	BBH	112 067
112 030	BBH	112 068
112 031	BBH	112 069
112 032	BBH	112 070
112 033	BBH	112 071
112 034	BBH	112 072
112 035	BBH	112 073
112 036	BBH	112 074
112 037	BBH	112 075
112 038	BBH	112 076
112 039	BBH	112 077

CLASS 113   Bo-Bo

Built: 1962-64 by Krauss-Maffei as class 110. Reclassified 1968.
System: 15 kV ac 16.67 Hz ac overhead.
Electrical Equipment: Siemens.

Continuous Rating: 3620 kW .
Weight: 86.0 tonnes.
Length: 16.490 m.
Maximum Speed: 160 km/h.
Train Heating: Electric (1000 V system).

CLASS 113.2 Original Body Design.

113 265 (112 265)	AH1	113 268 (112 268)	AH1
113 266 (112 266)	AH1	113 269 (112 269)	AH1
113 267 (112 267)	AH1	113 270 (112 270)	AH1

CLASS 113.3 Revised Body Design.

113 308 (112 308)	AH1	113 311 (112 311)	AH1
113 309 (112 309)	AH1	113 312 (112 312)	AH1
113 310 (112 310)	AH1		

CLASS 114   Bo-Bo

Built: 1968 by Krauss-Maffei as class 112. Reclassified 1988.
System: 15 kV ac 16.67 Hz ac overhead.
Electrical Equipment: Siemens.
Continuous Rating: 3620 kW.
Weight: 86.0 tonnes.
Length: 16.490 m.
Maximum Speed: 140 km/h.
Train Heating: Electric (1000 V system).

114 485 AH1	114 492 AH1	114 500 AH1
114 486 AH1	114 493 AH1	114 501 AH1
114 487 AH1	114 495 AH1	114 502 AH1
114 488 AH1	114 496 AH1	114 503 AH1
114 489 AH1	114 497 AH1	114 504 AH1
114 490 AH1	114 498 AH1	
114 491 AH1	114 499 AH1	

CLASS 120   Bo-Bo

Built: 1987-89 by Henschel/Krauss-Maffei/Krupp.
System: 15 kV ac 16.67 Hz ac overhead.
Electrical Equipment: BBC.
Continuous Rating: 5600 kW.
Weight: 83.2 tonnes.
Length: 19.200 m.
Maximum Speed: 200 km/h.
Train Heating: Electric (1000 V system).

▲ 114 491 at Bamberg with the 1130 Stuttgart-Dresden 05.07.91   (P. Lockwood)

▼ 120 122 heads through Fulda with an Inter City service 22.09.90   (D.W. Fickes)

120 101 NN2	120 121 NN2	120 141 NN2
120 102 NN2	120 122 NN2	120 142 NN2
120 103 NN2	120 123 NN2	120 143 NN2
120 104 NN2	120 124 NN2	120 144 NN2
120 105 NN2	120 125 NN2	120 145 NN2
120 106 NN2	120 126 NN2	120 146 NN2
120 107 NN2	120 127 NN2	120 147 NN2
120 108 NN2	120 128 NN2	120 148 NN2
120 109 NN2	120 129 NN2	120 149 NN2
120 110 NN2	120 130 NN2	120 150 NN2
120 111 NN2	120 131 NN2	120 151 NN2
120 112 NN2	120 132 NN2	120 152 NN2
120 113 NN2	120 133 NN2	120 153 NN2
120 114 NN2	120 134 NN2	120 154 NN2
120 115 NN2	120 135 NN2	120 155 NN2
120 116 NN2	120 136 NN2	120 156 NN2
120 117 NN2	120 137 NN2	120 157 NN2
120 118 NN2	120 138 NN2	120 158 NN2
120 119 NN2	120 139 NN2	120 159 NN2
120 120 NN2	120 140 NN2	120 160 NN2

CLASS 139   Bo-Bo

Built: 1959-65 by Henschel/Krauss-Maffei/Krupp.
System: 15 kV ac 16.67 Hz ac overhead.
Electrical Equipment: BBC/Siemens/AEG.
Continuous Rating: 3620 kW.
Weight: 84.6 tonnes.
Length: 16.490 m.
Maximum Speed: 110 km/h.
Train Heating: Electric (1000 V system).
Notes: p - Equipped for Push/Pull working.

139 131 p	RM	139 309 p	RM	139 554	MH1
139 132	MH1	139 310 p	RM	139 555	MH1
139 133	MH1	139 311 p	RM	139 556	MH1
139 135 p	RM	139 312 p	RM	139 557	MH1
139 136 p	RM	139 313 p	RM	139 558	MH1
139 137 p	RM	139 314 p	RM	139 559	MH1
139 163	MH1	139 315 p	RM	139 560	MH1
139 164	MH1	139 316 p	RM	139 561	MH1
139 165	MH1	139 552	MH1	139 562	MH1
139 166	RM	139 553	MH1	139 563	MH1

CLASS 140   Bo-Bo

Built: 1957-73 by Henschel/Krauss-Maffei/Krupp.
System: 15 kV ac 16.67 Hz ac overhead.
Electrical Equipment: BBC/Siemens/AEG.
Continuous Rating: 3620 kW.
Weight: 83.0 tonnes.
Length: 16.490 m.
Maximum Speed: 110 km/h.
Train Heating: Electric (1000 V system).
Notes: m - Equipped for multiple working. 140 776/777/793 are fitted with automatic couplings for use on freight services between Bremerhaven and Bremen.

140 001	MH1	140 033	MH1	140 065	MH1
140 002	MH1	140 034	MH1	140 066	MH1
140 003	MH1	140 035	MH1	140 067	MH1
140 004	MH1	140 036	MH1	140 068	MH1
140 005	MH1	140 037	MH1	140 069	MH1
140 006	MH1	140 038	MH1	140 070	MH1
140 007	MH1	140 039	MH1	140 071	MH1
140 008	MH1	140 040	MH1	140 072	MH1
140 009	MH1	140 041	MH1	140 073	MH1
140 010	MH1	140 042	MH1	140 074	MH1
140 011	MH1	140 043	MH1	140 075	MH1
140 012	MH1	140 044	MH1	140 076	MH1
140 013	MH1	140 045	MH1	140 077	MH1
140 014	MH1	140 046	MH1	140 078	MH1
140 015	MH1	140 047	MH1	140 079	RM
140 016	MH1	140 048	MH1	140 080	RM
140 017	MH1	140 049	MH1	140 081	RM
140 018	MH1	140 050	MH1	140 082	RM
140 019	MH1	140 051	MH1	140 083	RM
140 020	MH1	140 052	MH1	140 084	RM
140 021	MH1	140 053	MH1	140 085	RM
140 022	MH1	140 054	MH1	140 086	RM
140 023	MH1	140 055	MH1	140 087	RM
140 024	MH1	140 056	MH1	140 088	RM
140 025	MH1	140 057	MH1	140 089	RM
140 026	MH1	140 058	MH1	140 090	RM
140 027	MH1	140 059	MH1	140 091	RM
140 028	MH1	140 060	MH1	140 092	RM
140 029	MH1	140 061	MH1	140 093	RM
140 030	MH1	140 062	MH1	140 094	RM
140 031	MH1	140 063	MH1	140 095	RM
140 032	MH1	140 064	MH1	140 096	SSH

140 097	SSH	140 148	RM	140 197	RM
140 098	SSH	140 149	RM	140 198	RM
140 099	SSH	140 150	RM	140 199	KK
140 100	SSH	140 151	RM	140 200	KK
140 101	SSH	140 152	RM	140 201	KK
140 102	SSH	140 153	RM	140 202	KK
140 103	SSH	140 154	RM	140 203	KK
140 104	SSH	140 155	RM	140 204	KK
140 105	SSH	140 156	RM	140 205	KK
140 106	RM	140 157	RM	140 206	KK
140 107	RM	140 159	RM	140 207	KK
140 108	RM	140 160	RM	140 208	KK
140 109	RM	140 161	RM	140 209	KK
140 110	RM	140 162	RM	140 210	KK
140 111	RM	140 167	RM	140 211	RM
140 112	RM	140 168	RM	140 212	RM
140 113	RM	140 169	RM	140 213	RM
140 114	RM	140 170	RM	140 214	RM
140 115	RM	140 171	RM	140 215	RM
140 116	RM	140 172	RM	140 216	RM
140 117	RM	140 173	RM	140 217	RM
140 118	KK	140 174	HS	140 218	RM
140 119	KK	140 175	HS	140 219	RM
140 120	KK	140 176	HS	140 220	RM
140 121	KK	140 177	HS	140 221	RM
140 122	KK	140 178	SSH	140 222	RM
140 123	KK	140 179	SSH	140 223	RM
140 124	KK	140 180	SSH	140 224	RM
140 125	KK	140 181	SSH	140 225	RM
140 126	KK	140 182	RM	140 226	KK
140 127	KK	140 183	RM	140 227	KK
140 128	KK	140 184	RM	140 228	KK
140 129	KK	140 185	RM	140 229	KK
140 130	KK	140 186	RM	140 230	KK
140 138	RM	140 187	KK	140 231	KK
140 139	RM	140 188	KK	140 232	FF1
140 140	KK	140 189	KK	140 233	FF1
140 141	KK	140 190	KK	140 234	FF1
140 142	KK	140 191	MH1	140 235	FF1
140 143	KK	140 192	KK	140 236	FF1
140 144	KK	140 193	KK	140 237	FF1
140 145	RM	140 194	KK	140 238	FF1
140 146	RM	140 195 m	EDO	140 239	FF1
140 147	RM	140 196 m	EDO	140 240	FF1

▲ 139 136 at Singen 21.09.89   (R.G. Morris)

▼ 140 725 at Bw Bremerhaven 16.06.91   (G. Curtis)

140 241	FF1	140 285	EDO	140 337	KK
140 242	KK	140 286	EDO	140 338	KK
140 243	RM	140 287	EDO	140 339	KK
140 244	RM	140 288	EDO	140 340	KK
140 245	HS	140 289	EDO	140 341	KK
140 246	HS	140 290	MH1	140 342	KK
140 247	HS	140 291	KK	140 343	KK
140 248	KK	140 292	KK	140 344	KK
140 249	KK	140 293	KK	140 345	KK
140 250	KK	140 294	EDO	140 346	KK
140 251	RM	140 295	FB	140 347	KK
140 252	RM	140 296	EDO	140 348	KK
140 253	FF1	140 297	FB	140 349	KK
140 254	FF1	140 298	EDO	140 350	RM
140 255	EDO	140 299	FF1	140 351	KK
140 256	KK	140 300	FF1	140 352	KK
140 257	KK	140 301	FF1	140 353	KK
140 258	KK	140 302	FF1	140 354	KK
140 259	KK	140 303	FF1	140 355	RM
140 260	RM	140 304	FF1	140 356	RM
140 261	RM	140 305	FF1	140 357	KK
140 262	KK	140 306	HS	140 358	KK
140 263	KK	140 307	HS	140 359	KK
140 264	KK	140 308	FF1	140 360	RM
140 265	EDO	140 317	KK	140 361	RM
140 266	EDO	140 318	KK	140 362 m	HS
140 267	EDO	140 319	KK	140 363	RM
140 268	KK	140 320	KK	140 364	RM
140 269	KK	140 321	KK	140 365	RM
140 270	KK	140 322	KK	140 366	RM
140 271	RM	140 323	KK	140 367	HS
140 272	EDO	140 324	KK	140 368	HS
140 273	EDO	140 325	KK	140 369	HS
140 274	EDO	140 326	KK	140 370	HS
140 275	EDO	140 327	KK	140 371	HS
140 276	EDO	140 328	KK	140 372	HS
140 277	EDO	140 329	KK	140 373	HS
140 278	EDO	140 330	KK	140 374	HS
140 279	EDO	140 331	KK	140 375	HS
140 280	EDO	140 332	KK	140 376	HS
140 281	EDO	140 333	KK	140 377	HS
140 282	EDO	140 334	KK	140 378	HS
140 283	EDO	140 335	KK	140 379	HS
140 284	EDO	140 336	KK	140 380	HS

140 381	HS	140 425	HS	140 469	HS
140 382	HS	140 426	HS	140 470	HS
140 383	HS	140 427	HS	140 471	SSH
140 384	HS	140 428	HS	140 472	SSH
140 385	HS	140 429	HS	140 473	SSH
140 386	HS	140 430	EDO	140 474	SSH
140 387	HS	140 431	FF1	140 475	SSH
140 388	HS	140 432	EDO	140 476	SSH
140 389	HS	140 433	HS	140 477	SSH
140 390	HS	140 434	HS	140 478	SSH
140 391	HS	140 435	HS	140 479	SSH
140 392	HS	140 436	HS	140 480	SSH
140 393	KK	140 437	HS	140 481	SSH
140 394	KK	140 438	HS	140 482	RM
140 395	RM	140 439	HS	140 483	RM
140 396	RM	140 440	HS	140 484	RM
140 397	RM	140 441	HS	140 485	RM
140 398	RM	140 442	HS	140 486	RM
140 399	HS	140 443	HS	140 487	RM
140 400	HS	140 444	HS	140 488	RM
140 401	KK	140 445	HS	140 489	RM
140 402	KK	140 446	HS	140 490	RM
140 403	KK	140 447	RM	140 491	RM
140 404	KK	140 448	HS	140 492	RM
140 405	RM	140 449	KHS	140 493	RM
140 406	RM	140 450	HS	140 494	RM
140 407	RM	140 451	HS	140 495	RM
140 408	RM	140 452	HS	140 496	RM
140 409	HS	140 453	HS	140 497	RM
140 410	HS	140 454	HS	140 498	RM
140 411	HS	140 455	HS	140 499	RM
140 412	HS	140 456	HS	140 500	RM
140 413	HS	140 457	HS	140 501	RM
140 414	HS	140 458	HS	140 502	RM
140 415	EDO	140 459	HS	140 503	RM
140 416	EDO	140 460	RM	140 504	RM
140 417	EDO	140 461	RM	140 505	RM
140 418	EDO	140 462	HS	140 506	RM
140 419	HS	140 463	HS	140 507	RM
140 420	EDO	140 464	HS	140 508	RM
140 421	EDO	140 465	HS	140 509	RM
140 422	HS	140 466	HS	140 510	RM
140 423	HS	140 467	HS	140 511	RM
140 424	HS	140 468	HS	140 512	RM

140 513	RM	140 569	EDO	140 613	HS
140 514	RM	140 570	EDO	140 614	HS
140 515	RM	140 571	EDO	140 615	HS
140 516	RM	140 572	EDO	140 616	HS
140 517	RM	140 573	EDO	140 617	HS
140 518	RM	140 574	EDO	140 618	HS
140 519	RM	140 575	EDO	140 619	HS
140 520	HS	140 576	EDO	140 620	HS
140 521	HS	140 577	EDO	140 621	FB
140 522	HS	140 578	EDO	140 622	FB
140 523	HS	140 579	EDO	140 623	FB
140 524	HS	140 580	HS	140 624	HS
140 525	RM	140 581	HS	140 625	FB
140 526	HS	140 582	KK	140 626	FB
140 527	HS	140 583	KK	140 627	FB
140 528	HS	140 584	KK	140 628	HS
140 529	RM	140 585	FF1	140 629	FB
140 530	RM	140 586	FF1	140 630	HS
140 531	RM	140 587	FF1	140 631	KK
140 532	HS	140 588	KK	140 632	KK
140 533	HS	140 589	KK	140 634	SSH
140 534	HS	140 590	KK	140 635	HS
140 535	HS	140 591	KK	140 636	HS
140 536	HS	140 592	HS	140 637	HS
140 537	HS	140 593	HS	140 638	HS
140 538	HS	140 594	HS	140 639	HS
140 539	HS	140 595	KK	140 640	HS
140 540	HS	140 596	KK	140 641	HS
140 541	HO	140 597	KK	140 642	HS
140 542	HS	140 598	KK	140 643	SSH
140 543	HS	140 599	KK	140 644	KK
140 544	HS	140 600	EDO	140 645	KK
140 545	HS	140 601	SSH	140 646	KK
140 546	FB	140 602	FB	140 647	HS
140 547	HS	140 603	FB	140 648	HO
140 548	HS	140 604	FB	140 649	KK
140 549	HS	140 605	FB	140 650	KK
140 550	HS	140 606	FB	140 651	KK
140 551	HS	140 607	FB	140 652	KK
140 564	EDO	140 608	RM	140 653	HO
140 565	EDO	140 609	HS	140 654	HO
140 566	EDO	140 610	HS	140 655	HO
140 567	EDO	140 611	HS	140 656	HO
140 568	EDO	140 612	HS	140 657	HO

140 658	HO	140 702	KK	140 746		EDO
140 659	HO	140 703	AH1	140 747		EDO
140 660	HO	140 704	AH1	140 748		AH1
140 661	HO	140 705	HO	140 749		FF1
140 662	HO	140 706 m	EDO	140 750		FF1
140 663	HO	140 707	HO	140 751		FF1
140 664	HO	140 708	HO	140 752		EDO
140 665	FB	140 709	KK	140 753		KK
140 666	SSH	140 710	KK	140 754		EDO
140 667	FB	140 711	RM	140 755		KK
140 668	AH1	140 712	RM	140 756		KK
140 669	AH1	140 713	HO	140 757	m	HS
140 670	KK	140 714	HO	140 758	m	HS
140 671	KK	140 715	HO	140 759	m	HS
140 672	KK	140 716	HO	140 760	m	HS
140 673	KK	140 717	KK	140 761	m	HS
140 674	KK	140 718	KK	140 762	m	HS
140 675	KK	140 719	AH1	140 763	m	HS
140 676	KK	140 720	AH1	140 764	m	HS
140 677	RM	140 721	HO	140 765	m	HS
140 678	RM	140 722	HO	140 766	m	HS
140 679	RM	140 723	SSH	140 767	m	HS
140 680	RM	140 724	SSH	140 768	m	HS
140 681	RM	140 725	HO	140 769	m	HS
140 682	RM	140 726	EDO	140 770	m	HS
140 683	AH1	140 727	KK	140 771	m	HS
140 684	KK	140 728	KK	140 772	m	HS
140 685	HO	140 729	AH1	140 773	m	HS
140 686	HO	140 730	AH1	140 774	m	HS
140 687	HO	140 731	AH1	140 775	m	HS
140 688	HO	140 732	AH1	140 776	m	HS
140 689	HO	140 733	AH1	140 777	m	HS
140 690	KK	140 734	AH1	140 778	m	HS
140 691	HS	140 735	AH1	140 779	m	HS
140 692	HS	140 736	AH1	140 780	m	HS
140 693	HO	140 737	HS	140 781	m	HS
140 694	HO	140 738	HS	140 782	m	HS
140 695	HO	140 739	EDO	140 783	m	HS
140 696	HO	140 740	KK	140 784	m	HS
140 697	HO	140 741	KK	140 785	m	HS
140 698	HO	140 742	KK	140 786	m	HS
140 699	HO	140 743	KK	140 787	m	EDO
140 700	HO	140 744	EDO	140 788	m	EDO
140 701	HO	140 745	EDO	140 789	m	EDO

140 790	m	EDO	140 820	m	EDO	140 850	m	EDO
140 791	m	EDO	140 821	m	EDO	140 851	m	EDO
140 792	m	HS	140 822	m	EDO	140 852	m	EDO
140 793	m	HS	140 823	m	EDO	140 853	m	EDO
140 794	m	AH1	140 824	m	EDO	140 854	m	EDO
140 795	m	AH1	140 825	m	EDO	140 855	m	EDO
140 796	m	AH1	140 826	m	EDO	140 856	m	EDO
140 797	m	AH1	140 827	m	EDO	140 857	m	EDO
140 798	m	AH1	140 828	m	EDO	140 858	m	EDO
140 799	m	AH1	140 829	m	EDO	140 859	m	EDO
140 800	m	AH1	140 830	m	EDO	140 860	m	EDO
140 801	m	AH1	140 831	m	EDO	140 861	m	EDO
140 802	m	AH1	140 832	m	EDO	140 862	m	EDO
140 803	m	AH1	140 833	m	KK	140 863	m	EDO
140 804	m	AH1	140 834	m	KK	140 864	m	EDO
140 805	m	AH1	140 835	m	KK	140 865	m	SSH
140 806	m	AH1	140 836	m	KK	140 866	m	SSH
140 807	m	AH1	140 837	m	KK	140 867	m	EDO
140 808	m	AH1	140 838	m	KK	140 868	m	SSH
140 809	m	AH1	140 839	m	KK	140 869	m	SSH
140 810	m	AH1	140 840	m	KK	140 870	m	SSH
140 811	m	AH1	140 841	m	EDO	140 871	m	SSH
140 812	m	EDO	140 842	m	EDO	140 872	m	SSH
140 813	m	EDO	140 843	m	EDO	140 873	m	SSH
140 814	m	EDO	140 844	m	EDO	140 874	m	SSH
140 815	m	EDO	140 845	m	EDO	140 875	m	SSH
140 816	m	EDO	140 846	m	EDO	140 876	m	SSH
140 817	m	EDO	140 847	m	EDO	140 877	m	SSH
140 818	m	EDO	140 848	m	EDO	140 878	m	SSH
140 819	m	EDO	140 849	m	EDO	140 879	m	SSH

CLASS 141   Bo-Bo

Built: 1956-69 by Henschel/Krauss-Maffei/Krupp.
System: 15 kV ac 16.67 Hz ac overhead.
Electrical Equipment: BBC/Siemens/AEG.
Continuous Rating: 2310 kW.
Weight: 66.4 tonnes.
Length: 15.620 m.
Maximum Speed: 120 km/h.
Train Heating: Electric (1000 V system).
Notes: All equipped for multiple working/push-pull working.
t - Equipped with tdm push-pull for working Nürnberg S-Bahn services.
o - Equipped with tdm push-pull for one person operation of services in the Saarbrücken area.

▲ Differing liveries are sported by 141 025, 141 125 and 140 358 around the turntable at Bw Würzburg 22.09.90 (D.W. Fickes).

▼ 242 361 at Bw Berlin Schöneweide 12.04.91 (D. Rowland)

141 001	FF1	141 050	NN1	141 099	FF1
141 003	SSH	141 051	NN1	141 100	FF1
141 004	NN1	141 052	NN1	141 101	FF1
141 006	NN1	141 053	NN1	141 102	FF1
141 007	NN1	141 054	RM	141 103	FF1
141 008	NN1	141 055	HS	141 105	FF1
141 009	NN1	141 056	RM	141 106	FF1
141 010	SSH	141 057	RM	141 107	FF1
141 011	NN1	141 058	RM	141 108	FF1
141 012	NN1	141 059	NN1	141 109	FF1
141 013	NN1	141 060	RM	141 110	NN1
141 014	NN1	141 061	HS	141 111	SSH
141 016	NN1	141 062	NN1	141 112	SSH
141 017	NN1	141 063	RM	141 114	SSH
141 018	NN1	141 064	FF1	141 115	SSH
141 019	NN1	141 065	FF1	141 116	HS
141 020	SSH	141 066	FF1	141 117	SSH
141 021	NN1	141 067	FF1	141 118	SSH
141 022	RM	141 068	FF1	141 120	SSH
141 023	NN1	141 069	FF1	141 121	RM
141 024	NN1	141 070	FF1	141 122	NN1
141 025	NN1	141 071	HS	141 123	NN1
141 026	NN1	141 072	HS	141 124	NN1
141 027	NN1	141 073	FB	141 125	NN1
141 029	NN1	141 074	HS	141 126	NN1
141 030	NN1	141 075	HS	141 127	NN1
141 031	NN1	141 076	HS	141 128	NN1
141 032	NN1	141 078	RM	141 130	FF1
141 034	NN1	141 080	HS	141 131	RM
141 035	NN1	141 081	HS	141 132	HS
141 036	NN1	141 082	FF1	141 133	RM
141 037	NN1	141 083	HS	141 134	NN1
141 038	NN1	141 084	HS	141 135	RM
141 039	NN1	141 085	FF1	141 136	HS
141 040	NN1	141 086	FF1	141 137	FF1
141 041	NN1	141 088	HS	141 138	HS
141 042	SSH	141 089	FF1	141 139	FF1
141 043	NN1	141 090	HS	141 140	HS
141 044	FF1	141 091	FF1	141 141	HS
141 045	FF1	141 093	FF1	141 142	FF1
141 046	HS	141 094	HS	141 143	HS
141 047	FF1	141 095	FF1	141 144	FF1
141 048	FF1	141 097	FF1	141 145	FF1
141 049	FF1	141 098	FF1	141 146	HS

141 147	FF1	141 194	RM	141 240	FB
141 148	NN1	141 195	FF1	141 241	FB
141 149	FF1	141 196	FF1	141 242	FB
141 150	FF1	141 198	FF1	141 243	HS
141 151	FF1	141 199	FF1	141 244	FB
141 152	HS	141 200	FF1	141 245	HS
141 153	SSH	141 201	HS	141 246	HS
141 154	RM	141 202	HS	141 247	FB
141 155	HS	141 203	HS	141 248	EHG
141 156	FF1	141 204	EHG	141 249	EHG
141 157	EHG	141 205	FF1	141 250	FB
141 158	FF1	141 206	HS	141 251	FB
141 159	EHG	141 207	EHG	141 252	FB
141 161	HS	141 208	HS	141 253	RM
141 162	FF1	141 210	HS	141 254	HS
141 163	EHG	141 211	HS	141 255	HS
141 164	FF1	141 212	SSH	141 256	HS
141 165	HS	141 213	SSH	141 257	RM
141 166	HS	141 214	FF1	141 258	EHG
141 167	FF1	141 215	RM	141 259	FB
141 168	HS	141 216	RM	141 260	FB
141 169	HS	141 217	RM	141 261	HS
141 170	HS	141 218	NN1	141 262	FF1
141 171	HS	141 219	NN1	141 263	HS
141 172	HS	141 220	NN1	141 264	HS
141 173	HS	141 221	RM	141 265	FF1
141 174	FB	141 222	RM	141 266	HS
141 175	RM	141 223	EHG	141 267	RM
141 176	RM	141 224	RM	141 268	EHG
141 177	RM	141 225	FF1	141 269	HS
141 178	FB	141 226	FF1	141 270	EHG
141 179	FF1	141 227	FF1	141 271	RM
141 180	HS	141 228	FF1	141 272	EHG
141 182	HS	141 229	FF1	141 273	EHG
141 183	HS	141 230	FF1	141 274	EHG
141 184	FF1	141 231	FF1	141 275	EHG
141 185	FF1	141 232	FF1	141 276	FB
141 186	FF1	141 233	FF1	141 277	FB
141 187	FF1	141 234	FF1	141 278	FB
141 189	FF1	141 235	HS	141 280	FB
141 190	FF1	141 236	RM	141 281	FB
141 191	FF1	141 237	NN1	141 283	HS
141 192	FF1	141 238	NN1	141 284	HS
141 193	FF1	141 239	NN1	141 285	HS

141 286	EHG	141 330	EHG	141 375	NN1
141 287	EHG	141 331	EHG	141 376	NN1
141 288	EHG	141 332	EHG	141 377	NN1
141 289	EHG	141 333	HS	141 378	NN1
141 290	EHG	141 334	HS	141 379	NN1
141 291	FB	141 336	HS	141 380	EHG
141 292	HS	141 337	RM	141 381	NN1
141 293	FB	141 338	RM	141 382	NN1
141 294	EHG	141 339	RM	141 383	NN1
141 295	HS	141 340	HS	141 384	NN1
141 296	EHG	141 341	HS	141 385	FF1
141 297	EHG	141 342	HS	141 386	FF1
141 298	HS	141 343	HS	141 387	FF1
141 299	RM	141 344	HS	141 388	EHG
141 300	EHG	141 345	HS	141 389 o	SSH
141 301	EHG	141 346 o	SSH	141 390 o	SSH
141 302	EHG	141 347	SSH	141 391	EHG
141 303	EHG	141 348	SSH	141 392 o	SSH
141 304	EHG	141 349	HS	141 393 o	SSH
141 305	EHG	141 350	HS	141 394	EHG
141 306	EHG	141 351	HS	141 395	SSH
141 307	NN1	141 352	NN1	141 396	NN1
141 308	FB	141 353	HS	141 397	NN1
141 309	HS	141 354	FF1	141 398	NN1
141 310	HS	141 355	FF1	141 399	FF1
141 311	FB	141 356	NN1	141 400	SSH
141 312	FB	141 357	NN1	141 401	FF1
141 313	FB	141 358	NN1	141 402 o	SSH
141 314	FB	141 359	NN1	141 403	SSH
141 315	FB	141 360	NN1	141 404	FF1
141 316	FB	141 361	HS	141 405	FF1
141 317	FB	141 362	NN1	141 406	FF1
141 318	SSH	141 363	NN1	141 407 o	SSH
141 319	SSH	141 364	NN1	141 408 o	SSH
141 320	SSH	141 365	NN1	141 409 o	SSH
141 321	HS	141 366	NN1	141 410 o	SSH
141 322	HS	141 367	NN1	141 411 o	SSH
141 323	HS	141 368	FF1	141 412	EHG
141 324	HS	141 369	NN1	141 413	SSH
141 325	HS	141 370	NN1	141 414	AH1
141 326	EHG	141 371	NN1	141 415	EHG
141 327	EHG	141 372	NN1	141 416	EHG
141 328	HS	141 373	NN1	141 417	AH1
141 329	HS	141 374	NN1	141 417	EHG

141 419	AH1	141 430	AH1	141 441	NN1
141 420	HS	141 431	HS	141 442	NN1
141 421	AH1	141 432	HS	141 443	EHG
141 422	AH1	141 433	HS	141 444	EHG
141 423	AH1	141 434	EHG	141 445	EHG
141 424	AH1	141 435	EHG	141 446	EHG
141 425	AH1	141 436	NN1	141 447	EHG
141 426	AH1	141 437	NN1	141 448	EHG
141 427	AH1	141 438	NN1	141 449	EHG
141 428	AH1	141 439	NN1	141 450	EHG
141 429	SSH	141 440	NN1	141 451	EHG

CLASS 142   Bo-Bo

Built: 1963-76 by LEW.
System: 15 kV 16.67 Hz overhead.
Electrical Equipment: LEW.
Continuous Rating: 2740 kW.
Weight: 82.5 tonnes.
Length: 16.260 m.
Maximum Speed: 100 km/h.
Train Heating: Electric (1000 V system).
Notes: All equipped for multiple working/push-pull working.

CLASS 142.0. Standard Design.

142 001 (242 001)	DR	142 020 (242 020)	LM
142 002 (242 002)	DD	142 021 (242 021)	LLW
142 003 (242 003)	DR	142 022 (242 022)	LM
142 004 (242 004)	DD	142 023 (242 023)	LHP
142 005 (242 005)	DD	142 025 (242 025)	LLW
142 006 (242 006)	DD	142 026 (242 026)	LLW
142 007 (242 007)	DR	142 027 (242 027)	LM
142 008 (242 008)	DD	142 028 (242 028)	LHP
142 009 (242 009)	LLW	142 029 (242 029)	LLW
142 010 (242 010)	DR	142 030 (242 030)	LLW
142 011 (242 011)	DR	142 031 (242 031)	LLW
142 012 (242 012)	LM	142 032 (242 032)	LLW
142 013 (242 013)	LM	142 033 (242 033)	UW
142 014 (242 014)	LM	142 034 (242 034)	DR
142 015 (242 015)	LM	142 035 (242 035)	LHP
142 016 (242 016)	LHP	142 036 (242 036)	LLW
142 017 (242 017)	LLW	142 037 (242 037)	UW
142 018 (242 018)	LHP	142 038 (242 038)	LM
142 019 (242 019)	LM	142 039 (242 039)	LM

142 040 (242 040)	(Z)	142 087 (242 087)	LM
142 041 (242 041)	BP	142 088 (242 088)	LM
142 042 (242 042)	UW	142 089 (242 089)	UER
142 043 (242 043)	UW	142 090 (242 090)	BP
142 044 (242 044)	LWI	142 091 (242 091)	LM
142 045 (242 045)	LLW	142 092 (242 092)	LM
142 046 (242 046)	LLW	142 093 (242 093)	UW
142 047 (242 047)	LLW	142 094 (242 094)	LM
142 048 (242 048)	LLW	142 095 (242 095)	LM
142 049 (242 049)	LLW	142 096 (242 096)	LM
142 050 (242 050)	LWI	142 097 (242 097)	LM
142 051 (242 051)	LM	142 098 (242 098)	LWI
142 053 (242 053)	LHP	142 099 (242 099)	LM
142 054 (242 054)	LWI	142 100 (242 100)	BP
142 055 (242 055)	LLW	142 101 (242 101)	LM
142 056 (242 056)	LHP	142 102 (242 102)	LHP
142 057 (242 057)	UW	142 103 (242 103)	LWI
142 058 (242 058)	LHP	142 104 (242 104)	LLW
142 059 (242 059)	LHP	142 105 (242 105)	LLW
142 060 (242 060)	LM	142 106 (242 106)	LLW
142 061 (242 061)	LWI	142 107 (242 107)	LLW
142 062 (242 062)	LWI	142 108 (242 108)	LLW
142 063 (242 063)	LHP	142 109 (242 109)	LM
142 064 (242 064)	UW	142 110 (242 110)	LLW
142 065 (242 065)	UW	142 112 (242 112)	LHP
142 067 (242 067)	UW	142 113 (242 113)	LHP
142 068 (242 068)	LLW	142 114 (242 114)	LHP
142 069 (242 069)	LM	142 115 (242 115)	LHP
142 070 (242 070)	LM	142 116 (242 116)	LHP
142 071 (242 071)	UER	142 117 (242 117)	LHP
142 072 (242 072)	BP	142 118 (242 118)	LHP
142 074 (242 074)	LHP	142 119 (242 119)	LHP
142 075 (242 075)	LM	142 120 (242 120)	LHP
142 076 (242 076)	LHP	142 121 (242 121)	BP
142 077 (242 077)	LLW	142 122 (242 122)	LHP
142 078 (242 078)	LM	142 123 (242 123)	BP
142 079 (242 079)	LWI	142 124 (242 124)	LLW
142 080 (242 080)	LM	142 125 (242 125)	LHP
142 081 (242 081)	LM	142 126 (242 126)	UW
142 082 (242 082)	LM	142 127 (242 127)	LLW
142 083 (242 083)	LM	142 128 (242 128)	UW
142 084 (242 084)	LM	142 129 (242 129)	UW
142 085 (242 085)	LM	142 130 (242 130)	UER
142 086 (242 086)	BSN	142 132 (242 132)	UW

142 133 (242 133)	UW	142 177 (242 177)	DC
142 134 (242 134)	UW	142 178 (242 178)	LM
142 135 (242 135)	LM	142 179 (242 179)	BP
142 136 (242 136)	BP	142 180 (242 180)	BSN
142 137 (242 137)	BP	142 181 (242 181)	BP
142 138 (242 138)	UW	142 182 (242 182)	BP
142 139 (242 139)	BP	142 183 (242 183)	BSN
142 140 (242 140)	LM	142 184 (242 184)	DRI
142 141 (242 141)	LLW	142 185 (242 185)	BP
142 142 (242 142)	BBS	142 186 (242 186)	DR
142 143 (242 143)	LHP	142 187 (242 187)	DC
142 144 (242 144)	UA	142 188 (242 188)	BP
142 145 (242 145)	LM	142 189 (242 189)	BBS
142 146 (242 146)	DC	142 191 (242 191)	BSN
142 147 (242 147)	BP	142 193 (242 193)	DC
142 148 (242 148)	UER	142 194 (242 194)	BSN
142 149 (242 149)	LLW	142 195 (242 195)	DC
142 150 (242 150)	UA	142 196 (242 196)	BSN
142 151 (242 151)	UER	142 197 (242 197)	BP
142 152 (242 152)	BP	142 198 (242 198)	BSN
142 153 (242 153)	UER	142 199 (242 199)	BSN
142 154 (242 154)	UER	142 200 (242 200)	BBS
142 155 (242 155)	LHP	142 201 (242 201)	BSN
142 156 (242 156)	BP	142 203 (242 203)	BBS
142 157 (242 157)	UER	142 204 (242 204)	LHP
142 158 (242 158)	BBS	142 205 (242 205)	LHP
142 159 (242 159)	BP	142 206 (242 206)	LHP
142 160 (242 160)	LHP	142 207 (242 207)	LHP
142 161 (242 161)	BSN	142 208 (242 208)	LHP
142 162 (242 162)	BSN	142 209 (242 209)	LLW
142 163 (242 163)	BP	142 210 (242 210)	LLW
142 164 (242 164)	DR	142 211 (242 211)	LLW
142 165 (242 165)	DC	142 212 (242 212)	LLW
142 166 (242 166)	BSN	142 213 (242 213)	LLW
142 167 (242 167)	BP	142 214 (242 214)	LHP
142 168 (242 168)	BP	142 215 (242 215)	BJ
142 169 (242 169)	BP	142 216 (242 216)	DC
142 170 (242 170)	DD	142 217 (242 217)	DR
142 171 (242 171)	LLW	142 218 (242 218)	DR
142 172 (242 172)	DD	142 219 (242 219)	BJ
142 173 (242 173)	DC	142 220 (242 220)	DRI
142 174 (242 174)	LLW	142 221 (242 221)	DR
142 175 (242 175)	BSN	142 222 (242 222)	DR
142 176 (242 176)	BSN	142 224 (242 224)	DD

142 225 (242 225)	DRI		142 259 (242 259)	LWI
142 226 (242 226)	DRI		142 260 (242 260)	BBS
142 227 (242 227)	LHP		142 261 (242 261)	LHP
142 228 (242 228)	LWI		142 262 (242 262)	LHP
142 229 (242 229)	LWI		142 263 (242 263)	DR
142 230 (242 230)	DR		142 264 (242 264)	DRI
142 231 (242 231)	DRI		142 265 (242 265)	DRI
142 232 (242 232)	DRI		142 266 (242 266)	BJ
142 233 (242 233)	BJ		142 267 (242 267)	DD
142 234 (242 234)	BSN		142 268 (242 268)	DR
142 235 (242 235)	BJ		142 269 (242 269)	DRI
142 236 (242 236)	DRI		142 270 (242 270)	DC
142 237 (242 237)	DC		142 271 (242 271)	DC
142 238 (242 238)	DD		142 272 (242 272)	DC
142 239 (242 239)	DRI		142 273 (242 273)	BJ
142 240 (242 240)	DR		142 274 (242 274)	DC
142 241 (242 241)	DRI		142 275 (242 275)	BSN
142 242 (242 242)	DRI		142 276 (242 276)	DC
142 243 (242 243)	LWI		142 277 (242 277)	DC
142 244 (242 244)	LWI		142 278 (242 278)	DC
142 245 (242 245)	LWI		142 279 (242 279)	DC
142 246 (242 246)	LWI		142 280 (242 280)	DC
142 247 (242 247)	LWI		142 281 (242 281)	BSN
142 248 (242 248)	LWI		142 282 (242 282)	DR
142 249 (242 249)	LWI		142 283 (242 283)	DC
142 250 (242 250)	LWI		142 284 (242 284)	DC
142 251 (242 251)	LWI		142 285 (242 285)	DR
142 252 (242 252)	LWI		142 286 (242 286)	DR
142 253 (242 253)	LWI		142 287 (242 287)	DC
142 254 (242 254)	LWI		142 288 (242 288)	DC
142 255 (242 255)	LWI		142 289 (242 289)	DC
142 256 (242 256)	LWI		142 290 (242 290)	BJ
142 257 (242 257)	LWI		142 291 (242 291)	BJ
142 258 (242 258)	LWI		142 292 (242 292)	BJ

CLASS 142.3. Rebuilt 1985 onwards from Class 211.

142 310 (242 310)	LM		142 356 (242 356)	BBS
142 316 (242 316)	LM		142 363 (242 363)	BBS
142 337 (242 337)	BP		142 364 (242 364)	LLW
142 340 (242 340)	BBS		142 365 (242 365)	LM
142 341 (242 341)	BP		142 366 (242 366)	BBS
142 351 (242 351)	BBS		142 368 (242 368)	BBS
142 354 (242 354)	BBS		142 374 (242 374)	LLW
142 355 (242 355)	LM		142 376 (242 376)	LHP

▲ 143 648 (formerly 246 643) at Bw Leipzig West 01.01.92 (D.W. Fickes)

▼ 150 053 at Wanne Eickel 21.10.88 (R.G. Morris)

142 377 (242 377)	BBS		142 387 (242 387)	LM
142 378 (242 378)	LLW		142 393 (242 393)	LHP
142 381 (242 381)	LLW		142 395 (242 395)	LHP
142 383 (242 383)	BBS			

CLASS 143   Bo-Bo

Built: 1984-89 by LEW.
System: 15 kV 16.67 Hz overhead.
Electrical Equipment: LEW.
Continuous Rating: 3540 kW.
Weight: 82.0 tonnes.
Length: 16.640 m.
Maximum Speed: 120 km/h.
Train Heating: Electric (1000 V system).
Notes: All fitted with push-pull equipment.
** On loan to Schweizerische Sudostbahn.

CLASS 142.0 Standard Design.

143 002 (243 002)	LHP		143 030 (243 030)	CST
143 003 (243 003)	LHP		143 031 (243 031)	DR
143 005 (243 005)	LHP		143 032 (243 032)	LF
143 006 (243 006)	CP		143 033 (243 033)	DR
143 007 (243 007)	DR		143 034 (243 034)	LLW
143 008 (243 008)	DR		143 035 (243 035)	CST
143 009 (243 009)	UW		143 036 (243 036)	CST
143 010 (243 010)	UW		143 037 (243 037)	CST
143 011 (243 011)	LHP		143 038 (243 038)	DR
143 012 (243 012)	UW		143 039 (243 039)	CST
143 013 (243 013)	CST		143 040 (243 040)	CP
143 014 (243 014)	UW		143 041 (243 041)	DR
143 015 (243 015)	UW		143 042 (243 042)	BC
143 017 (243 017)	DR		143 043 (243 043)	CNZ
143 018 (243 018)	LHP		143 044 (243 044)	UW
143 019 (243 019)	CST		143 045 (243 045)	DR
143 020 (243 020)	CST		143 046 (243 046)	DR
143 021 (243 021)	DR		143 047 (243 047)	CST
143 022 (243 022)	DR		143 048 (243 048)	DR
143 023 (243 023)	UW		143 049 (243 049)	DR
143 024 (243 024)	DR		143 050 (243 050)	CST
143 025 (243 025)	CST		143 052 (243 052)	CST
143 026 (243 026)	DR		143 053 (243 053)	CNZ
143 027 (243 027)	LLW		143 054 (243 054)	BSG
143 028 (243 028)	CST		143 055 (243 055)	LHP
143 029 (243 029)	LLW		143 056 (243 056)	CWE

143 057 (243 057)	LLW		143 104 (243 104)	BC
143 058 (243 058)	LLW		143 105 (243 105)	LM
143 059 (243 059)	LLW		143 106 (243 106)	LM
143 061 (243 061)	CWE		143 107 (243 107)	CP
143 062 (243 062)	CP		143 108 (243 108)	DD
143 063 (243 063)	CP		143 109 (243 109)	BE
143 064 (243 064)	LF		143 110 (243 110)	CP
143 065 (243 065)	CWE		143 111 (243 111)	CNZ
143 066 (243 066)	CP		143 112 (243 112)	DD
143 067 (243 067)	CP		143 113 (243 113)	CNZ
143 068 (243 068)	LLW		143 114 (243 114)	LM
143 069 (243 069)	CP		143 115 (243 115)	LHP
143 070 (243 070)	CWE		143 116 (243 116)	CST
143 071 (243 071)	CWE		143 117 (243 117)	CP
143 072 (243 072)	CWE		143 118 (243 118)	BSG
143 073 (243 073)	CWE		143 119 (243 119)	LHP
143 074 (243 074)	LLW		143 120 (243 120)	LM
143 075 (243 075)	CWE		143 121 (243 121)	CR
143 076 (243 076)	CWE		143 122 (243 122)	CNZ
143 077 (243 077)	BC		143 123 (243 123)	LM
143 078 (243 078)	CST		143 124 (243 124)	BJ
143 079 (243 079)	DR		143 125 (243 125)	CNZ
143 080 (243 080)	CST		143 126 (243 126)	BC
143 081 (243 081)	DR		143 127 (243 127)	BH
143 082 (243 082)	CST		143 128 (243 128)	BJ
143 083 (243 083)	LF		143 129 (243 129)	CNZ
143 084 (243 084)	LHP		143 130 (243 130)	LM
143 085 (243 085)	DR		143 131 (243 131)	CNZ
143 086 (243 086)	BJ		143 132 (243 132)	BBH
143 087 (243 087)	LM		143 133 (243 133)	DD
143 088 (243 088)	CP		143 134 (243 134)	BH
143 089 (243 089)	UW		143 135 (243 135)	CNZ
143 090 (243 090)	DR		143 136 (243 136)	CP
143 091 (243 091)	CNZ		143 137 (243 137)	LM
143 092 (243 092)	LF		143 138 (243 138)	BH
143 093 (243 093)	CP		143 139 (243 139)	LM
143 094 (243 094)	CST		143 140 (243 140)	BE
143 095 (243 095)	CP		143 141 (243 141)	BC
143 097 (243 097)	CNZ		143 143 (243 143)	LM
143 098 (243 098)	LM		143 144 (243 144)	BC
143 100 (243 100)	LLW		143 145 (243 145)	CP
143 101 (243 101)	LM		143 146 (243 146)	LM
143 102 (243 102)	DD		143 147 (243 147)	CP
143 103 (243 103)	LM		143 148 (243 148)	LLW

143 149 (243 149)	CWE
143 150 (243 150)	LHP
143 151 (243 151)	LM
143 152 (243 152)	UER
143 153 (243 153)	BE
143 154 (243 154)	LM
143 155 (243 155)	LHP
143 156 (243 156)	LHP
143 157 (243 157)	BSG
143 158 (243 158)	UA
143 159 (243 159)	UA
143 160 (243 160)	CP
143 161 (243 161)	LM
143 162 (243 162)	CR
143 163 (243 163)	BC
143 164 (243 164)	CNZ
143 165 (243 165)	CP
143 166 (243 166)	CP
143 167 (243 167)	BE
143 168 (243 168)	UER
143 169 (243 169)	LM
143 170 (243 170)	CST
143 171 (243 171)	CP
143 172 (243 172)	LHP
143 173 (243 173)	CP
143 174 (243 174)	LHP
143 175 (243 175)	CWE
143 176 (243 176)	CP
143 177 (243 177)	CWE
143 178 (243 178)	LF
143 179 (243 179)	CWE
143 180 (243 180)	BC
143 181 (243 181)	CP
143 182 (243 182)	BE
143 183 (243 183)	CP
143 184 (243 184)	LM
143 185 (243 185)	BSG
143 186 (243 186)	CP
143 187 (243 187)	BE
143 188 (243 188)	CP
143 189 (243 189)	CNZ
143 190 (243 190)	BJ
143 191 (243 191)	BE
143 192 (243 192)	CP
143 193 (243 193)	UER
143 194 (243 194)	CWE
143 195 (243 195)	BE
143 196 (243 196)	BH
143 197 (243 197)	BE
143 198 (243 198)	DD
143 199 (243 199)	BC
143 200 (243 200)	LLW
143 201 (243 201)	BE
143 202 (243 202)	BE
143 203 (243 203)	CNZ
143 204 (243 204)	CP
143 205 (243 205)	LM
143 206 (243 206)	DD
143 207 (243 207)	CNZ
143 208 (243 208)	CP
143 210 (243 210)	BSG
143 211 (243 211)	DD
143 212 (243 212)	CR
143 213 (243 213)	CST
143 214 (243 214)	LM
143 215 (243 215)	LM
143 216 (243 216)	LM
143 217 (243 217)	DD
143 218 (243 218)	CP
143 220 (243 220)	BH
143 221 (243 221)	DD
143 222 (243 222)	BBH
143 224 (243 224)	BJ
143 225 (243 225)	UER
143 226 (243 226)	LM
143 227 (243 227)	CWE
143 228 (243 228)	BBH
143 229 (243 229)	LHP
143 230 (243 230)	BH
143 231 (243 231)	CP
143 232 (243 232)	CWE
143 233 (243 233)	CP
143 234 (243 234)	LM
143 235 (243 235)	CR
143 236 (243 236)	CR
143 237 (243 237)	CR
143 238 (243 238)	CWE
143 239 (243 239)	UER

143 240 (243 240)	UER	143 285 (243 285)	BE
143 241 (243 241)	CWE	143 286 (243 286)	CWE
143 242 (243 242)	CR	143 287 (243 287)	CNZ
143 243 (243 243)	DD	143 288 (243 288)	BH
143 244 (243 244)	CP	143 289 (243 289)	BH
143 245 (243 245)	CR	143 290 (243 290)	LF
143 246 (243 246)	BE	143 291 (243 291)	CP
143 247 (243 247)	CR	143 292 (243 292)	BC
143 248 (243 248)	BE	143 293 (243 293)	BC
143 249 (243 249)	BE	143 294 (243 294)	BH
143 250 (243 250)	CWE	143 295 (243 295)	BJ
143 251 (243 251)	CWE	143 296 (243 296)	(Z)
143 252 (243 252)	BBH	143 298 (243 298)	CNZ
143 253 (243 253)	LHP	143 299 (243 299)	CR
143 254 (243 254)	BJ	143 300 (243 300)	LLW
143 255 (243 255)	UER	143 301 (243 301)	DD
143 256 (243 256)	BH	143 302 (243 302)	UER
143 257 (243 257)	CR	143 303 (243 303)	LLW
143 258 (243 258)	CR	143 304 (243 304)	LLW
143 259 (243 259)	CR	143 305 (243 305)	UER
143 260 (243 260)	CR	143 306 (243 306)	LLW
143 261 (243 261)	CWE	143 307 (243 307)	CR
143 262 (243 262)	BE	143 308 (243 308)	CR
143 263 (243 263)	DD	143 309 (243 309)	LLW
143 265 (243 265)	BH	143 310 (243 310)	DD
143 266 (243 266)	LM	143 311 (243 311)	UER
143 267 (243 267)	CR	143 312 (243 312)	CR
143 268 (243 268)	DD	143 313 (243 313)	CR
143 269 (243 269)	CR	143 314 (243 314)	DD
143 270 (243 270)	CR	143 315 (243 315)	CR
143 271 (243 271)	CR	143 316 (243 316)	CR
143 272 (243 272)	CR	143 317 (243 317)	BC
143 273 (243 273)	DD	143 318 (243 318)	BJ
143 274 (243 274)	CR	143 319 (243 319)	UER
143 275 (243 275)	CR	143 320 (243 320)	CR
143 276 (243 276)	CR	143 321 (243 321)	CR
143 277 (243 277)	CR	143 323 (243 323)	CWE
143 278 (243 278)	CWE	143 324 (243 324)	CR
143 279 (243 279)	CR	143 325 (243 325)	DD
143 280 (243 280)	CR	143 326 (243 326)	BBH
143 281 (243 281)	CR	143 327 (243 327)	CR
143 282 (243 282)	CR	143 328 (243 328)	CR
143 283 (243 283)	BSG	143 329 (243 329)	UER
143 284 (243 284)	LF	143 330 (243 330)	BBH

143 331 (243 331) BC	143 555 (243 555) BC
143 332 (243 332) BBH	143 556 (243 556) EDO
143 333 (243 333) UER	143 557 (243 557) EDO
143 334 (243 334) BJ	143 558 (243 558) EDO
143 335 (243 335) CR	143 559 (243 559) EDO
143 336 (243 336) LLW	143 560 (243 560) EDO
143 337 (243 337) BBH	143 561 (243 561) EDO
143 338 (243 338) DD	143 562 (243 562) EDO
143 339 (243 339) BSG	143 563 (243 563) EDO
143 340 (243 340) LLW	143 564 (243 564) EDO
143 341 (243 341) DD	143 565 (243 565) EDO
143 342 (243 342) UER	143 566 (243 566) EDO
143 343 (243 343) CST	143 567 (243 567) EDO
143 344 (243 344) BSG	143 568 (243 568) EDO
143 345 (243 345) DD	143 569 (243 569) EDO
143 346 (243 346) CR	143 570 (243 570) EDO
143 347 (243 347) LLW	143 571 (243 571) EDO
143 348 (243 348) LHP	143 572 (243 572) EDO
143 349 (243 349) LHP	143 573 (243 573) EDO
143 350 (243 350) CWE	143 574 (243 574) EDO
143 351 (243 351) BC	143 575 (243 575) EDO
143 352 (243 352) LF	143 576 (243 576) EDO
143 353 (243 353) LF	143 577 (243 577) EDO
143 354 (243 354) LHP	143 578 (243 578) EDO
143 355 (243 355) DD	143 579 (243 579) EDO
143 356 (243 356) UER	143 580 (243 580) EDO
143 357 (243 357) LLW	143 581 (243 581) EDO
143 358 (243 358) LLW	143 582 (243 582) EDO
143 359 (243 359) DD	143 583 (243 583) EDO
143 360 (243 360) LM	143 584 (243 584) DD
143 361 (243 361) DD	143 585 (243 585) EDO
143 362 (243 362) DD	143 586 (243 586) EDO
143 363 (243 363) LM	143 587 (243 587) EDO
143 364 (243 364) BJ	143 588 (243 588) EDO
143 365 (243 365) DD	143 589 (243 589) EDO
143 366 (243 366) UER	143 590 (243 590) EDO
143 367 (243 367) DD	143 591 (243 591) EDO
143 368 (243 368) DD	143 592 (243 592) EDO
143 369 (243 369) LHP	143 593 (243 593) EDO
143 370 (243 370) LHP	143 594 (243 594) CWE
143 551 (243 551) EDO	143 595 (243 595) EDO
143 552 (243 552) EDO	143 596 (243 596) RM
143 553 (243 553) EDO	143 597 (243 597) EDO
143 554 (243 554) EDO	143 598 (243 598) LHP

143 599 (243 599)	CWE	143 631 (243 631)	CST
143 600 (243 600)	EDO	143 632 (243 632)	CR
143 601 (243 601)	CR	143 633 (243 633)	BJ
143 602 (243 602)	EDO	143 634 (243 634)	RM
143 603 (243 603)	CR	143 635 (243 635)	LHP
143 604 (243 604)	LLW	143 636 (243 636)	LHP
143 605 (243 605)	LLW	143 637 (243 637)	LHP
143 606 (243 606)	EDO	143 638 (243 638)	LLW
143 607 (243 607)	EDO	143 639 (243 639)	BJ
143 608 (243 608)	EDO	143 640 (243 640)	CR
143 609 (243 609)	EDO	143 641 (243 641)	BC
143 610 (243 610)	CST	143 642 (243 642)	BC
143 611 (243 611)	UER	143 643 (243 643)	BC
143 612 (243 612)	EDO	143 644 (243 644)	BBH
143 613 (243 613)	EDO	143 645 (243 645)	LHP
143 614 (243 614)	EDO	143 646 (243 646)	LLW
143 615 (243 615)	EDO	143 647 (243 647)	BBH
143 616 (243 616)	BBH	143 648 (243 648)	LLW
143 617 (243 617)	EDO	143 649 (243 649)	BBH
143 618 (243 618)	EDO	143 650 (243 650)	BBH
143 619 (243 619)	EDO	143 651 (243 651)	BC
143 620 (243 620)	CR	143 652 (243 652)	BC
143 621 (243 621)	BJ	143 653 (243 653)	BC
143 622 (243 622)	(Z)	143 654 (243 654)	BC
143 623 (243 623)	BJ	143 655 (243 655)	BBH
143 624 (243 624)	EDO	143 656 (243 656)	BBH
143 625 (243 625)	EDO	143 657 (243 657)	BBH
143 626 (243 626)	EDO	143 658 (243 658)	UER
143 627 (243 627)	BJ	143 659 (243 659)	RM
143 628 (243 628)	RM	143 660 (243 660)	CR
143 629 (243 629)	RM	143 661 (243 661)	CP
143 630 (243 630)	CST	143 662 (243 662)	CWE

CLASS 143.8 Equipped for multiple working.

143 801 (243 801)	BJ	143 812 (243 812)	LF
143 802 (243 802)	CWE	143 813 (243 813)	LF
143 803 (243 803)	DD	143 814 (243 814)	LF
143 804 (243 804)	DD	143 815 (243 815)	LHP
143 805 (243 805)	DD	143 816 (243 816)	LHP
143 806 (243 806)	DD	143 817 (243 817)	LHP
143 807 (243 807)	BJ	143 818 (243 818)	BSG
143 808 (243 808)	CWE	143 819 (243 819)	FK
143 809 (243 809)	LLW	143 820 (243 820)	BC
143 810 (243 810)	BSG	143 821 (243 821)	BSG
143 811 (243 811)	DD	143 822 (243 822)	LM

143 823 (243 823)	BC	143 867 (243 867)	DD
143 824 (243 824)	DD	143 868 (243 868)	CWE
143 825 (243 825)	LHP	143 869 (243 869)	BSG
143 826 (243 826)	UER	143 870 (243 870)	CST
143 827 (243 827)	CNZ	143 871 (243 871)	EDO
143 828 (243 828)	LM	143 872 (243 872)	RM
143 829 (243 829)	BBH	143 873 (243 873)	EDO
143 830 (243 830)	CST	143 874 (243 874)	CST
143 831 (243 831)	BJ	143 875 (243 875)	DD
143 832 (243 832)	DD	143 876 (243 876)	RM
143 833 (243 833)	LF	143 877 (243 877)	EDO
143 834 (243 834)	BJ	143 878 (243 878)	EDO
143 835 (243 835)	BSG	143 879 (243 879)	EDO
143 836 (243 836)	CST	143 880 (243 880)	EDO
143 837 (243 837)	BSG	143 881 (243 881)	EDO
143 838 (243 838)	CST	143 882 (243 882)	EDO
143 839 (243 839)	CWE	143 883 (243 883)	RM
143 840 (243 840)	LLW	143 884 (243 884)	EDO
143 841 (243 841)	LLW	143 885 (243 885)	RM
143 842 (243 842)	CNZ	143 886 (243 886)	CR
143 843 (243 843)	BJ	143 887 (243 887)	EDO
143 844 (243 844)	BJ	143 888 (243 888)	EDO
143 845 (243 845)	CNZ	143 889 (243 889)	EDO
143 846 (243 846)	DD	143 890 (243 890)	RM
143 847 (243 847)	DD	143 891 (243 891)	EDO
143 848 (243 848)	BSG	143 892 (243 892)	EDO
143 849 (243 849)	BBH	143 893 (243 893)	VER
143 850 (243 850)	BBH	143 894 (243 894)	EDO
143 851 (243 851)	BBH	143 895 (243 895)	EDO
143 852 (243 852)	BBH	143 896 (243 896)	RM
143 853 (243 853)	LLW	143 897 (243 897)	RM
143 854 (243 854)	LLW	143 898 (243 898)	EDO
143 855 (243 855)	LLW	143 899 (243 899)	RM
143 856 (243 856)	LLW	143 900 (243 900)	EDO
143 857 (243 857)	LLW	143 901 (243 901)	EDO
143 858 (243 858)	LLW	143 902 (243 902)	RM
143 859 (243 859)	CNZ	143 903 (243 903)	EDO
143 860 (243 860)	CST	143 904 (243 904)	RM
143 861 (243 861)	LHP	143 905 (243 905)	RM
143 862 (243 862)	CWE	143 906 (243 906)	RM
143 863 (243 863)	LLW	143 907 (243 907)	EDO
143 864 (243 864)	LLW	143 908 (243 908)	RM
143 865 (243 865)	BSG	143 909 (243 909)	EDO
143 866 (243 866)	BC	143 910 (243 910)	EDO

143 911 (243 911)	EDO		143 943 (243 943)	EDO
143 913 (243 913)	EDO		143 944 (243 944)	EDO
143 914 (243 914)	RM		143 945 (243 945)	EDO
143 915 (243 915)	RM		143 946 (243 946)	EDO
143 916 (243 916)	RM		143 947 (243 947)	EDO
143 917 (243 917)	EDO		143 948 (243 948)	EDO
143 918 (243 918)	EDO		143 949 (243 949)	EDO
143 919 (243 919)	EDO		143 950 (243 950)	EDO
143 920 (243 920)	RM		143 951 (243 951)	EDO
143 921 (243 921)	EDO		143 952 (243 952)	RM
143 922 (243 922)	**		143 953 (243 953)	BC
143 923 (243 923)	RM		143 954 (243 954)	RM
143 924 (243 924)	EDO		143 955 (243 955)	EDO
143 925 (243 925)	RM		143 956 (243 956)	BSG
143 926 (243 926)	RM		143 957 (243 957)	EDO
143 927 (243 927)	RM		143 958 (243 958)	EDO
143 928 (243 928)	EDO		143 959 (243 959)	EDO
143 929 (243 929)	RM		143 960 (243 960)	EDO
143 930 (243 930)	RM		143 961 (243 961)	EDO
143 931 (243 931)	BC		143 962 (243 962)	RM
143 932 (243 932)	EDO		143 963 (243 963)	EDO
143 933 (243 933)	EDO		143 964 (243 964)	EDO
143 934 (243 934)	RM		143 965 (243 965)	EDO
143 935 (243 935)	RM		143 966 (243 966)	LHP
143 936 (243 936)	EDO		143 967 (243 967)	EDO
143 937 (243 937)	EDO		143 968 (243 968)	EDO
143 938 (243 938)	BJ		143 969 (243 969)	BSG
143 939 (243 939)	EDO		143 970 (243 970)	CST
143 940 (243 940)	EDO		143 971 (243 971)	CST
143 941 (243 941)	BJ		143 972 (243 972)	CWE
143 942 (243 942)	EDO		143 973 (243 973)	DD

CLASS 150   Co-Co

Built: 1957-73 by Krupp.
System: 15 kV ac 16.67 Hz ac overhead.
Electrical Equipment: AEG.
Continuous Rating: 4410 kW.
Weight: 128 tonnes (* 126 tonnes)
Length: 19.490 m.
Maximum Speed: 100 km/h.
Train Heating: Electric (1000 V system).

150 001*NN2	150 004*NN2	150 007*NN2
150 002*NN2	150 005*NN2	150 008*NN2
150 003*NN2	150 006*NN2	150 009*NN2

150 010* NN2	150 055 TS	150 100 NN2
150 011* NN2	150 056 EHG	150 101 NN2
150 012* NN2	150 057 EHG	150 102 NN2
150 013* NN2	150 058 EHG	150 103 NN2
150 014* NN2	150 059 EHG	150 104 NN2
150 015* NN2	150 060 EHG	150 105 NN2
150 016* NN2	150 061 TS	150 106 EHG
150 017* NN2	150 062 TS	150 107 EHG
150 018* NN2	150 063 NN2	150 108 EHG
150 019* NN2	150 064 NN2	150 109 EHG
150 020* NN2	150 065 NN2	150 110 EHG
150 021* NN2	150 066 NN2	150 111 EHG
150 022* NN2	150 067 NN2	150 112 EHG
150 023* NN2	150 068 NN2	150 113 TS
150 024* NN2	150 070 NN2	150 114 TS
150 025* NN2	150 071 NN2	150 115 TS
150 026 NN2	150 072 NN2	150 116 TS
150 027 NN2	150 073 NN2	150 117 TS
150 028 NN2	150 074 NN2	150 118 TS
150 029 NN2	150 075 NN2	150 119 TS
150 030 NN2	150 076 NN2	150 120 EHG
150 031 NN2	150 077 NN2	150 121 EHG
150 032 NN2	150 078 NN2	150 122 EHG
150 033 NN2	150 079 NN2	150 123 EHG
150 034 NN2	150 080 NN2	150 124 EHG
150 035 NN2	150 081 NN2	150 125 EHG
150 036 NN2	150 082 NN2	150 126 EHG
150 037 NN2	150 083 NN2	150 127 EHG
150 038 NN2	150 084 NN2	150 128 EHG
150 039 NN2	150 085 NN2	150 129 EHG
150 040 NN2	150 086 NN2	150 130 EHG
150 041 NN2	150 087 NN2	150 131 EHG
150 042 NN2	150 088 NN2	150 132 EHG
150 043 NN2	150 089 NN2	150 133 EHG
150 044 NN2	150 090 NN2	150 134 EHG
150 045 EHG	150 091 NN2	150 135 EHG
150 046 EHG	150 092 NN2	150 136 EHG
150 047 EHG	150 093 NN2	150 137 EHG
150 049 EHG	150 094 NN2	150 138 EHG
150 050 EHG	150 095 NN2	150 139 EHG
150 051 EHG	150 096 NN2	150 140 EHG
150 052 EHG	150 097 NN2	150 141 EHG
150 053 EHG	150 098 NN2	150 142 EHG
150 054 EHG	150 099 NN2	150 143 TS

▲ 151 098 at Bw Bremen 4 16.06.91 (G. Curtis)

▼ 155 053 (formerly 250 053) at Bw Leipzig West on 01.01.92 (D.W. Fickes)

150 144 TS	150 161 TS	150 178 TS
150 145 TS	150 162 TS	150 179 TS
150 146 TS	150 163 TS	150 180 TS
150 147 TS	150 164 TS	150 181 TS
150 148 TS	150 165 TS	150 182 TS
150 149 TS	150 166 TS	150 183 TS
150 150 TS	150 167 TS	150 184 TS
150 151 TS	150 168 TS	150 185 TS
150 152 TS	150 169 TS	150 186 TS
150 153 TS	150 170 TS	150 187 TS
150 154 TS	150 171 TS	150 188 TS
150 155 TS	150 172 TS	150 189 TS
150 156 TS	150 173 TS	150 190 TS
150 157 TS	150 174 TS	150 191 TS
150 158 TS	150 175 TS	150 192 TS
150 159 TS	150 176 TS	150 193 TS
150 160 TS	150 177 TS	150 194 TS

CLASS 151   Co-Co

Built: 1973-77 by Krupp.
System: 15 kV ac 16.67 Hz ac overhead.
Electrical Equipment: AEG.
Continuous Rating: 5982 kW.
Weight: 118 tonnes.
Length: 19.490 m.
Maximum Speed: 120 km/h.
Train Heating: Electric (1000 V system).
Notes: All equipped for multiple working/push-pull working.

a - Equipped with automatic couplings for use on Hamburg-Peine & Duisburg-Ehrang/Saar iron ore trains.

151 001	NN2	151 014	NN2	151 027	NN2
151 002	NN2	151 015	NN2	151 028	NN2
151 003	NN2	151 016	NN2	151 029	NN2
151 004	NN2	151 017	NN2	151 030	NN2
151 005	NN2	151 018	NN2	151 031	NN2
151 006	NN2	151 019	NN2	151 032	NN2
151 007	NN2	151 020	NN2	151 033	NN2
151 008	NN2	151 021	NN2	151 034	NN2
151 009	NN2	151 022	NN2	151 035	NN2
151 010	NN2	151 023	NN2	151 036	NN2
151 011	NN2	151 024	NN2	151 037	NN2
151 012	NN2	151 025	NN2	151 038	NN2
151 013	NN2	151 026	NN2	151 039	NN2

151 040	NN2	151 084	NN2	151 128	EHG
151 041	NN2	151 085	NN2	151 129	EHG
151 042	NN2	151 086	NN2	151 130	EHG
151 043	NN2	151 087	NN2	151 131	EHG
151 044	NN2	151 088	NN2	151 132	EHG
151 045	NN2	151 089 a	EHG	151 133	EHG
151 046	NN2	151 090 a	EHG	151 134	EHG
151 047	NN2	151 091 a	EHG	151 135	EHG
151 048	NN2	151 092 a	EHG	151 136	EHG
151 049	NN2	151 093 a	EHG	151 137	EHG
151 050	NN2	151 094 a	EHG	151 138	EHG
151 051	NN2	151 095 a	EHG	151 139	EHG
151 052	NN2	151 096 a	EHG	151 140	EHG
151 053	NN2	151 097 a	EHG	151 141	EHG
151 054	NN2	151 098 a	EHG	151 142	EHG
151 055	NN2	151 099 a	EHG	151 143	EHG
151 056	NN2	151 100	NN2	151 144	EHG
151 057	NN2	151 101	NN2	151 145	EHG
151 058	NN2	151 102	NN2	151 146	EHG
151 059	NN2	151 103	NN2	151 147	EHG
151 060	NN2	151 104	NN2	151 148	EHG
151 061	NN2	151 105	EHG	151 149	EHG
151 062	NN2	151 106	EHG	151 150	EHG
151 063	NN2	151 107	EHG	151 151	EHG
151 064	NN2	151 108	EHG	151 152	EHG
151 065	NN2	151 109	EHG	151 153	EHG
151 066	NN2	151 110	EHG	151 154	EHG
151 067	NN2	151 111	EHG	151 155	EHG
151 068	NN2	151 112	EHG	151 156	EHG
151 069	NN2	151 113	EHG	151 157	EHG
151 070	NN2	151 114 a	EHG	151 158	EHG
151 071	NN2	151 115 a	EHG	151 159	EHG
151 072	NN2	151 116 a	EHG	151 160	EHG
151 073	NN2	151 117 a	EHG	151 161	EHG
151 074	NN2	151 118 a	EHG	151 162	EHG
151 075	NN2	151 119 a	EHG	151 163	EHG
151 076	NN2	151 120 a	EHG	151 164	EHG
151 077	NN2	151 121 a	EHG	151 165	EHG
151 078	NN2	151 122 a	EHG	151 166	EHG
151 079	NN2	151 123	EHG	151 167	EHG
151 080	NN2	151 124	EHG	151 168	EHG
151 081	NN2	151 125	EHG	151 169	EHG
151 082	NN2	151 126	EHG	151 170	EHG
151 083	NN2	151 127	EHG		

CLASS 155   Co-Co

Built: 1974-84 by LEW.
System: 15 kV 16.67 Hz overhead.
Electrical Equipment: LEW.
Continuous Rating: 5100 kW.
Weight: 123.0 tonnes.
Length: 19.600 m.
Maximum Speed: 125 km/h.
Train Heating: Electric (1000 V system).
Notes: ** On loan to Schweizerische Sudostbahn.

155 001 (250 001)	LHP		155 035 (250 035)	BSN
155 003 (250 003)	LHP		155 036 (250 036)	LF
155 004 (250 004)	BE		155 037 (250 037)	DR
155 005 (250 005)	DC		155 038 (250 038)	LF
155 006 (250 006)	BE		155 039 (250 039)	DC
155 007 (250 007)	LLW		155 040 (250 040)	LHP
155 008 (250 008)	LHP		155 041 (250 041)	LLW
155 009 (250 009)	DC		155 042 (250 042)	LHP
155 010 (250 010)	DC		155 043 (250 043)	LLW
155 011 (250 011)	DR		155 044 (250 044)	LF
155 012 (250 012)	BSN		155 045 (250 045)	LHP
155 013 (250 013)	LLW		155 046 (250 046)	LHP
155 014 (250 014)	DC		155 047 (250 047)	LHP
155 015 (250 015)	LLW		155 048 (250 048)	DR
155 016 (250 016)	DR		155 049 (250 049)	DD
155 017 (250 017)	LHP		155 050 (250 050)	DC
155 018 (250 018)	LF		155 051 (250 051)	BC
155 019 (250 019)	BC		155 052 (250 052)	LHP
155 020 (250 020)	LF		155 053 (250 053)	LLW
155 021 (250 021)	LF		155 054 (250 054)	DRI
155 022 (250 022)	BSG		155 055 (250 055)	LLW
155 023 (250 023)	LLW		155 056 (250 056)	BH
155 024 (250 024)	LLW		155 057 (250 057)	LLW
155 025 (250 025)	DRI		155 058 (250 058)	LHP
155 026 (250 026)	DR		155 059 (250 059)	DD
155 027 (250 027)	LLW		155 060 (250 060)	LLW
155 028 (250 028)	BSN		155 061 (250 061)	LHP
155 029 (250 029)	LLW		155 062 (250 062)	LLW
155 030 (250 030)	BSN		155 063 (250 063)	BH
155 031 (250 031)	DRI		155 064 (250 064)	DR
155 032 (250 032)	LLW		155 065 (250 065)	LHP
155 033 (250 033)	DR		155 066 (250 066)	LHP
155 034 (250 034)	DR		155 067 (250 067)	BSG

155 068 (250 068)	LF
155 069 (250 069)	BE
155 070 (250 070)	DRI
155 071 (250 071)	LLW
155 072 (250 072)	DRI
155 073 (250 073)	BSN
155 074 (250 074)	BSN
155 075 (250 075)	DR
155 076 (250 076)	LHP
155 077 (250 077)	LHP
155 078 (250 078)	LF
155 079 (250 079)	DR
155 080 (250 080)	BSN
155 081 (250 081)	DC
155 082 (250 082)	BSN
155 083 (250 083)	BC
155 084 (250 084)	BSN
155 085 (250 085)	NN2
155 086 (250 086)	LHP
155 087 (250 087)	DC
155 088 (250 088)	BSN
155 089 (250 089)	UW
155 090 (250 090)	BE
155 091 (250 091)	BSN
155 092 (250 092)	LHP
155 093 (250 093)	BE
155 094 (250 094)	DR
155 095 (250 095)	DR
155 096 (250 096)	LHP
155 097 (250 097)	BE
155 098 (250 098)	BSN
155 099 (250 099)	BH
155 100 (250 100)	BC
155 101 (250 101)	BSN
155 102 (250 102)	BC
155 103 (250 103)	LF
155 104 (250 104)	LF
155 105 (250 105)	LLW
155 107 (250 107)	DD
155 108 (250 108)	LLW
155 109 (250 109)	BH
155 110 (250 110)	BSG
155 111 (250 111)	BC
155 112 (250 112)	DR
155 113 (250 113)	DD
155 114 (250 114)	LF
155 115 (250 115)	BSG
155 116 (250 116)	DC
155 117 (250 117)	DRI
155 118 (250 118)	LF
155 119 (250 119)	LLW
155 120 (250 120)	LF
155 121 (250 121)	LF
155 122 (250 122)	LHP
155 123 (250 123)	BSG
155 124 (250 124)	LF
155 125 (250 125)	LLW
155 126 (250 126)	LLW
155 127 (250 127)	DC
155 128 (250 128)	BH
155 129 (250 129)	LHP
155 130 (250 130)	DR
155 131 (250 131)	LLW
155 132 (250 132)	LLW
155 133 (250 133)	LLW
155 134 (250 134)	BC
155 135 (250 135)	UW
155 136 (250 136)	UW
155 137 (250 137)	BC
155 138 (250 138)	BSN
155 139 (250 139)	BSN
155 140 (250 140)	BSN
155 141 (250 141)	DD
155 142 (250 142)	DD
155 143 (250 143)	DD
155 144 (250 144)	DD
155 146 (250 146)	BSN
155 147 (250 147)	BSN
155 148 (250 148)	BSN
155 149 (250 149)	BSN
155 150 (250 150)	DC
155 151 (250 151)	BSN
155 152 (250 152)	BSN
155 153 (250 153)	DD
155 154 (250 154)	DD
155 155 (250 155)	BSN
155 156 (250 156)	BSN
155 157 (250 157)	BSN

155 158 (250 158)	DD	
155 159 (250 159)	BSN	
155 160 (250 160)	BSN	
155 161 (250 161)	BSN	
155 162 (250 162)	LLW	
155 163 (250 163)	LHP	
155 164 (250 164)	LHP	
155 165 (250 165)	LLW	
155 166 (250 166)	LHP	
155 167 (250 167)	BSN	
155 168 (250 168)	UW	
155 169 (250 169)	DR	
155 170 (250 170)	BSN	
155 171 (250 171)	BSN	
155 172 (250 172)	BSN	
155 173 (250 173)	DD	
155 174 (250 174)	BSN	
155 175 (250 175)	UW	
155 176 (250 176)	LHP	
155 177 (250 177)	LHP	
155 178 (250 178)	LF	
155 179 (250 179)	LLW	
155 180 (250 180)	UW	
155 181 (250 181)	BSN	
155 182 (250 182)	DR	
155 183 (250 183)	UW	
155 184 (250 184)	LLW	
155 185 (250 185)	LLW	
155 186 (250 186)	DC	
155 187 (250 187)	LHP	
155 188 (250 188)	BH	
155 189 (250 189)	LF	
155 190 (250 190)	DD	
155 191 (250 191)	DD	
155 192 (250 192)	DD	
155 193 (250 193)	DD	
155 194 (250 194)	LHP	
155 195 (250 195)	NN2	
155 196 (250 196)	BSN	
155 197 (250 197)	LHP	
155 198 (250 198)	LHP	
155 199 (250 199)	LLW	
155 200 (250 200)	DC	
155 201 (250 201)	BC	
155 202 (250 202)	DC	
155 203 (250 203)	LF	
155 204 (250 204)	LHP	
155 205 (250 205)	UW	
155 206 (250 206)	DD	
155 207 (250 207)	NN2	
155 208 (250 208)	DC	
155 209 (250 209)	BSG	
155 210 (250 210)	UW	
155 211 (250 211)	LLW	
155 212 (250 212)	UER	
155 213 (250 213)	BC	
155 214 (250 214)	DR	
155 215 (250 215)	UER	
155 216 (250 216)	LF	
155 217 (250 217)	DC	
155 218 (250 218)	DR	
155 219 (250 219)	DR	
155 220 (250 220)	UER	
155 221 (250 221)	LLW	
155 222 (250 222)	DC	
155 223 (250 223)	LHP	
155 224 (250 224)	DD	
155 225 (250 225)	DD	
155 226 (250 226)	LF	
155 227 (250 227)	DC	
155 228 (250 228)	UER	
155 229 (250 229)	DC	
155 230 (250 230)	BC	
155 231 (250 231)	BH	
155 232 (250 232)	LHP	
155 233 (250 233)	BC	
155 234 (250 234)	BC	
155 235 (250 235)	LHP	
155 236 (250 236)	LLW	
155 237 (250 237)	NN2	
155 238 (250 238)	LHP	
155 239 (250 239)	LHP	
155 240 (250 240)	BC	
155 241 (250 241)	LHP	
155 242 (250 242)	UW	
155 243 (250 243)	NN2	
155 244 (250 244)	LHP	
155 245 (250 245)	LHP	

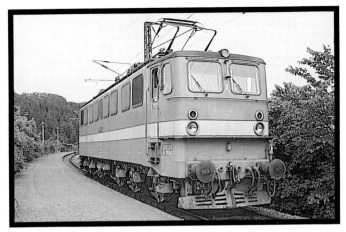

▲ The Blankenburg to Königshütte line is electrified at 25 kV. 251 001 stands at Braunesumph 16.07.91 (D.W. Fickes)

▼ 181 220 at Luxembourg 26.06.89 (J. Hayes)

155 246 (250 246)	BSN		155 260 (250 260)	LHP
155 247 (250 247)	BC		155 261 (250 261)	NN2
155 248 (250 248)	LF		155 262 (250 262)	LHP
155 249 (250 249)	LHP		155 263 (250 263)	LHP
155 250 (250 250)	DC		155 264 (250 264)	NN2
155 251 (250 251)	UER		155 265 (250 265)	UER
155 252 (250 252)	**		155 266 (250 266)	LHP
155 253 (250 253)	BC		155 267 (250 267)	LHP
155 254 (250 254)	UER		155 268 (250 268)	NN2
155 255 (250 255)	BSG		155 269 (250 269)	BSG
155 256 (250 256)	LHP		155 270 (250 270)	LLW
155 257 (250 257)	LF		155 271 (250 271)	LLW
155 258 (250 258)	LHP		155 272 (250 272)	BSG
155 259 (250 259)	LHP		155 273 (250 273)	UER

CLASS 156   Co-Co

Built: 1991 onwards by LEW.
System: 15 kV 16.67 Hz overhead.
Electrical Equipment: LEW.
Continuous Rating: 5880 kW.
Weight:
Length: 19.500 m.
Maximum Speed: 120 km/h.
Train Heating: Electric (1000 V system).
Note: Trial locomotives owned by LEW on loan to DR.

156 001 (252 001)	LKP	156 003 (252 003)	
156 002 (252 002)		156 004 (252 004)	

CLASS 171   Co-Co

Built: 1964-65 by LEW.
System: 25 kV 50 Hz overhead.
Electrical Equipment: LEW.
Continuous Rating: 3300 kW.
Weight: 126.0 tonnes.
Length: 18.640 m.
Maximum Speed: 80 km/h.
Train Heating: Electric (1000 V system).

171 001 (251 001)	LB	171 006 (251 006)	LB
171 002 (251 002)	LB	171 007 (251 007)	LB
171 003 (251 003)	LB	171 008 (251 008)	LB
171 004 (251 004)	LB	171 009 (251 009)	LB
171 005 (251 005)	LB	171 010 (251 010)	LB

171 011 (251 011)	LB		171 014 (251 014)	LB
171 012 (251 012)	LB		171 015 (251 015)	LB
171 013 (251 013)	LB			

CLASS 180   Bo-Bo

Built: 1987-91 by Skoda.
System: 15 kV 16.67 Hz overhead/3 kV dc overhead.
Electrical Equipment: Skoda.
Continuous Rating:
Weight: 84.0 tonnes.
Length: 16.800 m.
Maximum Speed: 120 km/h.
Train Heating: Electric (1000 V system).

180 001 (230 001)	DD	180 011 (230 011)	DD
180 002 (230 002)	DD	180 012 (230 012)	DD
180 003 (230 003)	DD	180 013 (230 013)	DD
180 004 (230 004)	DD	180 014 (230 014)	DD
180 005 (230 005)	DD	180 015 (230 015)	DD
180 006 (230 006)	DD	180 016 (230 016)	DD
180 007 (230 007)	DD	180 017 (230 017)	DD
180 008 (230 008)	DD	180 018 (230 018)	DD
180 009 (230 009)	DD	180 019 (230 019)	DD
180 010 (230 010)	DD	180 020 (230 020)	DD

CLASS 181   Bo-Bo

Built: 1974-75 (* 1967) by Krupp.
System: 15 kV ac 16.67 Hz ac overhead/25 Kv ac 50 Hz overhead.
Electrical Equipment: AEG.
Continuous Rating: 3200 kW (* 3000 kW).
Weight: 82.5 tonnes (* 84.0 tonnes).
Length: 17.940 m. (* 16.950 m.).
Maximum Speed: 160 km/h (* 150 km/h).
Train Heating: Electric (1000 V system).
Notes: All equipped for multiple working/push-pull working.

181 001*	SSH	181 205	SSH
181 104*	SSH	181 206	SSH
181 201	SSH	181 207	SSH
181 202	SSH	181 208	SSH
181 203	SSH	181 209	SSH
181 204	SSH	181 210	SSH

181 211 SSH	Lorraine
181 212 SSH	Luxembourg
181 213 SSH	Saar
181 214 SSH	Mosel
181 215 SSH	
181 216 SSH	
181 217 SSH	
181 218 SSH	
181 219 SSH	
181 220 SSH	
181 221 SSH	
181 222 SSH	
181 223 SSH	
181 224 SSH	
181 225 SSH	

CLASS 184   Bo-Bo

Built: 1966 by Krupp.
System: 15 kV ac 16.67 Hz ac overhead/25 Kv ac 50 Hz overhead.
Electrical Equipment: AEG.
Continuous Rating: 3000 kW.
Weight: 84.0 tonnes.
Length: 16.950 m.
Maximum Speed: 150 km/h.
Train Heating: Electric (1000 V system).
Notes: Built as quad-voltage locomotives also able to operate on 3000 V dc overhead/1500 V dc overhead. Circuitry amended to as shown above in 1979. All equipped for multiple working/push-pull working.

184 001 SSH   184 002 SSH   184 003 SSH

BATTERY ELECTRIC LOCOMOTIVES

CLASS 381   B

Built: 1938 by Windhoff/Siemens.
Battery: 6 GiS 400 of 360 A/h.
Weight: 17.0 tonnes.
Length: 6.45 m.
Maximum Speed: 25 km/h.

381 020 FF2

▲ 184 002 stabled at Ehrang 19.04.87 (B.A. Hawkins)

▼ 401 556 leaves Hannover Hbf 18.06.91 (A.J. Marshall)

CLASS 382   B

Built: 1955 by Gmeinder/Garbe-Lahmeyer.
Battery: 6 GiS 400 of 360 A/h.
Weight: 21.0 tonnes.
Length: 6.432 m.
Maximum Speed: 30 km/h.

382 001 AOP

ELECTRIC MULTIPLE UNITS

CLASS 401   IC-EXPRESS

Built: 1989-91 by Krupp/Krauss-Maffei/Henschel.
System: 15 kV ac 16.67 Hz ac overhead.
Electrical Equipment: Siemens/ABB/AEG.
Continuous Rating: 4800 kW.
Wheel Arrangement: Bo-Bo.
Weight: 78.0 (* 75.5) tonnes.
Length: 20.560 m.
Maximum Speed: 280 km/h.

CLASS 401.00 Thyristor control.

401 001 AH1	401 008 AH1	401 015 AH1
401 002 AH1	401 009 AH1	401 016 AH1
401 003 AH1	401 010 AH1	401 017 AH1
401 004 AH1	401 011 AH1	401 018 AH1
401 005 AH1	401 012 AH1	401 019 AH1
401 006 AH1	401 013 AH1	401 020 AH1
401 007 AH1	401 014 AH1	

CLASS 401.05 GTO-Thyristor control.

401 051* AH1	401 058* AH1	401 065* AH1
401 052* AH1	401 059* AH1	401 066* AH1
401 053* AH1	401 060* AH1	401 067* AH1
401 054* AH1	401 061* AH1	401 068* AH1
401 055* AH1	401 062* AH1	401 069* AH1
401 056* AH1	401 063* AH1	401 070* AH1
401 057* AH1	401 064* AH1	401 071* AH1

▲ A Class 403/4 Lufthansa airport passes through the Düsseldorf suburbs on 13.05.88
(D.J. Glossop).

▼ The class 410/810 5-car IC Experimental unit at Fulda on a special train to Würzburg
29.05.88 (D.J. Glossop)

CLASS 401.5 Thyristor control.

401 501 AH1	401 508 AH1	401 515 AH1
401 502 AH1	401 509 AH1	401 516 AH1
401 503 AH1	401 510 AH1	401 517 AH1
401 504 AH1	401 511 AH1	401 518 AH1
401 505 AH1	401 512 AH1	401 519 AH1
401 506 AH1	401 513 AH1	401 520 AH1
401 507 AH1	401 514 AH1	

CLASS 401.55 GTO-Thyristor control.

401 551* AH1	401 558* AH1	401 565* AH1
401 552* AH1	401 559* AH1	401 566* AH1
401 553* AH1	401 560* AH1	401 567* AH1
401 554* AH1	401 561* AH1	401 568* AH1
401 555* AH1	401 562* AH1	401 569* AH1
401 556* AH1	401 563* AH1	401 570* AH1
401 557* AH1	401 564* AH1	401 571* AH1

CLASSES 403/404   AIRPORT EXPRESS

Built: 1973 by LHB/MAN/MBB.
System: 15 kV ac 16.67 Hz ac overhead.
Electrical Equipment: AEG/BBC/Siemens.
Continuous Rating: 960 kW per car.
Wheel Arrangement: Bo-Bo + Bo-Bo + Bo-Bo + Bo-Bo.
Weight: 235.7 tonnes.
Length: 27.450 + 27.160 + 27.160 + 27.450 m.
Maximum Speed: 200 km/h.
Seats: 45F + 51F + 42F + 45F.
Notes: On hire to Lufthansa for workings between Düsseldorf Flughafen and Frankfurt (Main) Flughafen.

403 001	404 001	404 101	403 002	KD
403 003	404 002	404 102	403 004	KD
403 005	404 003	404 103	403 006	KD

CLASSES 410   IC-EXPERIMENTAL

Built: 1986 by Krupp/Henschel (Power Cars), MAN Trailers.
System: 15 kV ac 16.67 Hz ac overhead.
Electrical Equipment: Siemens.
Continuous Rating: 4200 kW.
Wheel Arrangement: Bo-Bo + 2-2 + 2-2 + 2-2 + Bo-Bo.

Weight: 78.2 + 51 + 51 + 51 + 78.2 tonnes.
Length: 20.810 + 24.340 + 24.340 + 24.340 + 20.810 m.
Maximum Speed: 350 km/h.
Seats: 0 + 36F + 24F, 27S + 0 + 0.

410 001 810 001 810 002 810 003 410 002 FF1

CLASSES 420/421   3-CAR UNITS

Built: 1969-90 by LHB/MBB/O & K/Uerdingen/Waggon Union.
System: 15 kV ac 16.67 Hz ac overhead.
Electrical Equipment: AEG/BBC/Siemens.
Continuous Rating: 800 kW per car.
Wheel Arrangements: Bo-Bo + Bo-Bo + Bo-Bo.
Weights: 44 + 41 + 44 tonnes.
Length: 23.300 + 20.800 + 23.300 m.
Maximum Speed: 120 km/h.
Seats: 63S + 17F 49S + 65S.
Notes: * Additional luggage space for working to and from München Flughafen. Seating capapcities not available at the time of going to press. A number of new replacement cars have been constructed to replace accident damaged vehicles as follows: 420 132 (original withdrawn 29.01.81, new car to service 01.11.81), 421 042 (30.11.87, 04.08.89), 421 093 (30.11.87, 29.08.89), 421 140 (29.04.82, 20.02.90), 421 150 (31.03.88, 11.10.89), 421 194 (28.02.85, 06.11.89), 421 219 (30.11.83, 21.11.89), 421 238 (30.08.88, 04.12.89), 421 263 (29.01.81, 11.12.89), 421 327 (30.11.87, 30.06.89). The new 420 132 was renumbered to 420 316 on 01.02.84, with 420 140 being renumbered 420 132 on the same date. 420 637 and 420 640 changed identities with effect from 01.02.84. 420 710 and 421 210 were renumbered 420 708 and 421 230 respectively on 17.08.90. A replacement 420 140 was delivered on 20.02.90.

420 001 421 001 420 501 MH6
420 002 421 002 420 502 MH6
420 003 421 003 420 503 MH6
420 004 421 004 420 504 MH6
420 005 421 005 420 505 MH6
420 006 421 006 420 506 MH6
420 007 421 007 420 507 MH6
420 008 421 008 420 508 MH6
420 009 421 009 420 509 MH6
420 010 421 010 420 510 MH6
420 011 421 011 420 511 MH6
420 012 421 012 420 512 MH6
420 013 421 013 420 513 MH6

420 014	421 014	420 514	MH6
420 015	421 015	420 515	MH6
420 016	421 016	420 516	MH6
420 017	421 017	420 517	MH6
420 018	421 018	420 518	MH6
420 019	421 019	420 519	MH6
420 020	421 020	420 520	MH6
420 021	421 021	420 521	MH6
420 022	421 022	420 522	MH6
420 023	421 023	420 523	MH6
420 024	421 024	420 524	MH6
420 025	421 025	420 525	MH6
420 026	421 026	420 526	MH6
420 027	421 027	420 527	MH6
420 028	421 028	420 528	MH6
420 029	421 029	420 529	MH6
420 030	421 030	420 530	MH6
420 031	421 031	420 531	MH6
420 032	421 032	420 532	MH6
420 033	421 033	420 533	MH6
420 034	421 034	420 534	MH6
420 035	421 035	420 535	MH6
420 036	421 036	420 536	MH6
420 037	421 037	420 537	MH6
420 038	421 038	420 538	MH6
420 039	421 039	420 539	MH6
420 040	421 040	420 540	MH6
420 041	421 041	420 541	MH6
420 042	421 042	420 542	MH6
420 043	421 043	420 543	MH6
420 044	421 044	420 544	MH6
420 045	421 045	420 545	MH6
420 046	421 046	420 546	MH6
420 047	421 047	420 547	MH6
420 048	421 048	420 548	MH6
420 049	421 049	420 549	MH6
420 050	421 050	420 550	MH6
420 051	421 051	420 551	MH6
420 052	421 052	420 552	MH6
420 053	421 053	420 553	MH6
420 054	421 054	420 554	MH6
420 055	421 055	420 555	MH6
420 056	421 056	420 556	MH6
420 057	421 057	420 557	MH6

```
420 058  421 058  420 558  MH6
420 059  421 059  420 559  MH6
420 060  421 060  420 560  MH6
420 061  421 061  420 561  MH6
420 062  421 062  420 562  MH6
420 063  421 063  420 563  MH6
420 064  421 064  420 564  MH6
420 065  421 065  420 565  MH6
420 066  421 066  420 566  MH6
420 067  421 067  420 567  MH6
420 068  421 068  420 568  MH6
420 069  421 069  420 569  MH6
420 070  421 070  420 570  MH6
420 071  421 071  420 571  MH6
420 072  421 072  420 572  MH6
420 073  421 073  420 573  MH6
420 074  421 074  420 574  MH6
420 075  421 075  420 575  MH6
420 076  421 076  420 576  MH6
420 077  421 077  420 577  MH6
420 078  421 078  420 578  MH6
420 079  421 079  420 579  MH6
420 080  421 080  420 580  MH6
420 081  421 081  420 581  MH6
420 082  421 082  420 582  MH6
420 083  421 083  420 583  MH6
420 084  421 084  420 584  MH6
420 085  421 085  420 585  MH6
420 086  421 086  420 586  MH6
420 087  421 087  420 587  MH6
420 088  421 088  420 588  MH6
420 089  421 089  420 589  MH6
420 090  421 090  420 590  MH6
420 091  421 091  420 591  MH6
420 092  421 092  420 592  MH6
420 093  421 093  420 593  MH6
420 094  421 094  420 594  MH6
420 095  421 095  420 595  MH6
420 096  421 096  420 596  MH6
420 097  421 097  420 597  MH6
420 098  421 098  420 598  MH6
420 099  421 099  420 599  MH6
420 100  421 100  420 600  MH6
420 101  421 101  420 601  MH6
```

420 102 421 102 420 602 MH6
420 103 421 103 420 603 MH6
420 104 421 104 420 604 MH6
420 105 421 105 420 605 MH6
420 106 421 106 420 606 MH6
420 107 421 107 420 607 MH6
420 108 421 108 420 608 MH6
420 109 421 109 420 609 MH6
420 110 421 110 420 610 MH6
420 111 421 111 420 611 MH6
420 112 421 112 420 612 MH6
420 113 421 113 420 613 MH6
420 114 421 114 420 614 MH6
420 115 421 115 420 615 MH6
420 116 421 116 420 616 MH6
420 117 421 117 420 617 MH6
420 118 421 118 420 618 MH6
420 119 421 119 420 619 MH6
420 120 421 120 420 620 MH6
420 121 421 121 420 621 MH6
420 122 421 122 420 622 MH6
420 123 421 123 420 623 MH6
420 124 421 124 420 624 MH6
420 125 421 125 420 625 MH6
420 126 421 126 420 626 MH6
420 127 421 127 420 627 MH6
420 128 421 128 420 628 MH6
420 129 421 129 420 629 MH6
420 130 421 130 420 630 MH6
420 131 421 131 420 631 MH6
420 132 421 132 420 632 MH6
420 133 421 133 420 633 MH6
420 134 421 134 420 634 MH6
420 135 421 135 420 635 MH6
420 136 421 136 420 636 MH6
420 137 421 137 420 637 MH6
420 138 421 138 420 638 MH6
420 139 421 139 420 639 MH6
420 140 421 140 420 640 MH6
420 141 421 141 420 641 MH6
420 142 421 142 420 642 MH6
420 143 421 143 420 643 MH6
420 144 421 144 420 644 MH6
420 145 421 145 420 645 MH6

```
420 146  421 146  420 646  MH6
420 147  421 147  420 647  MH6
420 148  421 148  420 648  MH6
420 149  421 149  420 649  MH6
420 150  421 150  420 650  MH6
420 151  421 151  420 651  MH6
420 152  421 152  420 652  MH6
420 153  421 153  420 653  MH6
420 154  421 154  420 654  MH6
420 155  421 155  420 655  MH6
420 156  421 156  420 656  MH6
420 157  421 157  420 657  MH6
420 158  421 158  420 658  MH6
420 159  421 159  420 659  MH6
420 160  421 160  420 660  MH6
420 161  421 161  420 661  MH6
420 162  421 162  420 662  MH6
420 163  421 163  420 663  MH6
420 164  421 164  420 664  MH6
420 165  421 165  420 665  MH6
420 166  421 166  420 666  MH6
420 167  421 167  420 667  MH6
420 168  421 168  420 668  MH6
420 169  421 169  420 669  MH6
420 170  421 170  420 670  MH6
420 171  421 171  420 671  MH6
420 172  421 172  420 672  MH6
420 173  421 173  420 673  MH6
420 174* 421 174* 420 674* MH6
420 175* 421 175* 420 675* MH6
420 176* 421 176* 420 676* MH6
420 177* 421 177* 420 677* MH6
420 178* 421 178* 420 678* MH6
420 179* 421 179* 420 679* MH6
420 180* 421 180* 420 680* MH6
420 181* 421 181* 420 681* MH6
420 182* 421 182* 420 682* MH6
420 183* 421 183* 420 683* MH6
420 184* 421 184* 420 684* MH6
420 185* 421 185* 420 685* MH6
420 186* 421 186* 420 686* MH6
420 187* 421 187* 420 687* MH6
420 188* 421 188* 420 688* MH6
420 189  421 189  420 689  MH6
```

```
420 190  421 190  420 690  MH6
420 191  421 191  420 691  FF1
420 192  421 192  420 692  FF1
420 193  421 193  420 693  FF1
420 194  421 194  420 694  MH6
420 195  421 195  420 695  MH6
420 196  421 196  420 696  FF1
420 197  421 197  420 697  FF1
420 198  421 198  420 698  FF1
420 199  421 199  420 699  FF1
420 200  421 200  420 700  FF1
420 201  421 201  420 701  FF1
420 202  421 202  420 702  FF1
420 203  421 203  420 703  FF1
420 204  421 204  420 704  FF1
420 205  421 205  420 705  FF1
420 206  421 206  420 706  FF1
420 207  421 207  420 707  FF1
420 208  421 208  420 708  FF1
420 209  421 209  420 709  FF1
420 211  421 211  420 711  FF1
420 212  421 212  420 712  FF1
420 213  421 213  420 713  FF1
420 214  421 214  420 714  FF1
420 215  421 215  420 715  FF1
420 216  421 216  420 716  FF1
420 217  421 217  420 717  FF1        Friedberg
420 218  421 218  420 718  FF1
420 219  421 219  420 719  FF1
420 220  421 220  420 720  FF1
420 221  421 221  420 721  FF1
420 222  421 222  420 722  FF1
420 223  421 223  420 723  FF1
420 224  421 224  420 724  FF1
420 225  421 225  420 725  FF1
420 226  421 226  420 726  FF1
420 227  421 227  420 727  FF1
420 228  421 228  420 728  FF1
420 229  421 229  420 729  FF1
420 230  421 230  420 730  FF1
420 231  421 231  420 731  FF1
420 232  421 232  420 732  FF1
420 233  421 233  420 733  FF1
420 234  421 234  420 734  FF1
```

420 235	421 235	420 735	FF1	
420 236	421 236	420 736	FF1	Wiesbaden
420 237	421 237	420 737	FF1	
420 238	421 238	420 738	FF1	
420 239	421 239	420 739	FF1	
420 240	421 240	420 740	FF1	
420 241	421 241	420 741	FF1	
420 242	421 242	420 742	FF1	
420 243	421 243	420 743	FF1	
420 244	421 244	420 744	FF1	
420 245	421 245	420 745	FF1	
420 246	421 246	420 746	FF1	Niedernhausen
420 247	421 247	420 747	FF1	
420 248	421 248	420 748	FF1	
420 249	421 249	420 749	FF1	
420 250	421 250	420 750	FF1	
420 251	421 251	420 751	FF1	Kronberg
420 252	421 252	420 752	FF1	Friedrichsdorf
420 253	421 253	420 753	FF1	Bad Soden
420 254	421 254	420 754	FF1	
420 255	421 255	420 755	FF1	
420 256	421 256	420 756	FF1	
420 257	421 257	420 757	FF1	
420 258	421 258	420 758	FF1	
420 259	421 259	420 759	FF1	
420 260	421 260	420 760	FF1	
420 261	421 261	420 761	FF1	
420 262	421 262	420 762	FF1	
420 263	421 263	420 763	FF1	
420 264	421 264	420 764	FF1	
420 265	421 265	420 765	FF1	
420 266	421 266	420 766	FF1	
420 267	421 267	420 767	FF1	
420 268	421 268	420 768	FF1	
420 269	421 269	420 769	FF1	
420 270	421 270	420 770	FF1	Schwalbach
420 271	421 271	420 771	FF1	Hofheim
420 272	421 272	420 772	FF1	Hochheim
420 273	421 273	420 773	FF1	Bad Homburg
420 274	421 274	420 774	FF1	Bad Vibel
420 275	421 275	420 775	FF1	Flörsheim am Main
420 276	421 276	420 776	FF1	Eschborn
420 277	421 277	420 777	FF1	Sulzbach
420 278	421 278	420 778	FF1	Oberursel

420 279	421 279	420 779	FF1	Frankfurt
420 280	421 280	420 780	FF1	Karben
420 281	421 281	420 781	FF1	Eppstein
420 282	421 282	420 782	FF1	Kriftel
420 283	421 283	420 783	FF1	Lorsbach
420 284	421 284	420 784	FF1	Höchst
420 285	421 285	420 785	FF1	Mainz
420 286	421 286	420 786	FF1	Niederjosbach
420 287	421 287	420 787	FF1	Dortelweil
420 288	421 288	420 788	FF1	Ludwigsburg
420 289	421 289	420 789	KD	
420 290	421 290	420 790	KD	
420 291	421 291	420 791	FF1	
420 292	421 292	420 792	FF1	
420 293	421 293	420 793	KD	
420 294	421 294	420 794	FF1	
420 295	421 295	420 795	FF1	
420 296	421 296	420 796	FF1	
420 297	421 297	420 797	FF1	
420 298	421 298	420 798	FF1	
420 299	421 299	420 799	TP	
420 300	421 300	420 800	FF1	
420 301	421 301	420 801	FF1	
420 302	421 302	420 802	TP	
420 303	421 303	420 803	TP	
420 304	421 304	420 804	TP	
420 305	421 305	420 805	TP	Plochingen
420 306	421 306	420 806	KD	
420 307	421 307	420 807	KD	
420 308	421 308	420 808	KD	
420 309	421 309	420 809	TP	
420 310	421 310	420 810	TP	
420 311	421 311	420 811	TP	
420 312	421 312	420 812	TP	
420 313	421 313	420 813	TP	
420 314	421 314	420 814	TP	
420 315	421 315	420 815	TP	
420 316	421 316	420 816	KD	
420 317	421 317	420 817	TP	
420 318	421 318	420 818	TP	
420 319	421 319	420 819	TP	
420 320	421 320	420 820	TP	
420 321	421 321	420 821	KD	
420 322	421 322	420 822	KD	

420 323	421 323	420 823	KD
420 324	421 324	420 824	TP
420 325	421 325	420 825	TP
420 326	421 326	420 826	TP
420 327	421 327	420 827	TP
420 328	421 328	420 828	TP
420 329	421 329	420 829	TP
420 330	421 330	420 830	TP
420 331	421 331	420 831	TP
420 332	421 332	420 832	TP
420 333	421 333	420 833	TP
420 334	421 334	420 834	TP
420 335	421 335	420 835	TP
420 336	421 336	420 836	TP
420 337	421 337	420 837	TP
420 338	421 338	420 838	TP
420 339	421 339	420 839	TP
420 340	421 340	420 840	TP
420 341	421 341	420 841	TP
420 342	421 342	420 842	TP
420 343	421 343	420 843	TP
420 344	421 344	420 844	TP
420 345	421 345	420 845	TP
420 346	421 346	420 846	TP
420 347	421 347	420 847	TP
420 348	421 348	420 848	TP
420 349	421 349	420 849	TP
420 350	421 350	420 850	TP
420 351	421 351	420 851	TP
420 352	421 352	420 852	TP
420 353	421 353	420 853	TP
420 354	421 354	420 854	TP
420 355	421 355	420 855	TP
420 356	421 356	420 856	TP
420 357	421 357	420 857	TP
420 358	421 358	420 858	TP
420 359	421 359	420 859	TP
420 360	421 360	420 860	TP
420 361	421 361	420 861	TP
420 362	421 362	420 862	TP
420 363	421 363	420 863	TP
420 364	421 364	420 864	TP
420 365	421 365	420 865	TP
420 366	421 366	420 866	TP

Waiblingen

```
420 367  421 367  420 867  TP
420 368  421 368  420 868  TP
420 369  421 369  420 869  TP
420 370  421 370  420 870  TP
420 371  421 371  420 871  TP
420 372  421 372  420 872  TP
420 373  421 373  420 873  TP
420 374  421 374  420 874  TP
420 375  421 375  420 875  TP
420 376  421 376  420 876  TP
420 377  421 377  420 877  TP
420 378  421 378  420 878  TP
420 379  421 379  420 879  TP
420 380  421 380  420 880  TP
420 381  421 381  420 881  TP
420 382  421 382  420 882  TP
420 383  421 383  420 883  TP
420 384  421 384  420 884  TP
420 385  421 385  420 885  TP
420 386  421 386  420 886  TP
420 387  421 387  420 887  TP
420 388  421 388  420 888  TP
420 389  421 389  420 889  TP          Bad Canstatt
420 390  421 390  420 890  TP
420 400  421 400  420 900  TP
420 401  421 401  420 901  TP
420 402  421 402  420 902  TP
420 403  421 403  420 903  TP
420 404  421 404  420 904  TP
420 405  421 405  420 905  TP
420 406  421 406  420 906  TP
420 407  421 407  420 907  TP
420 408  421 408  420 908  TP
420 409  421 409  420 909  TP
420 410  421 410  420 910  TP
420 411  421 411  420 911  TP
420 412  421 412  420 912  TP
420 413  421 413  420 913  TP
420 414  421 414  420 914  TP
420 415  421 415  420 915  TP
420 416  421 416  420 916  TP
420 417  421 417  420 917  TP
420 418  421 418  420 918  TP
420 419  421 419  420 919  TP
```

▲ EMU 420 308 + 421 308 + 420 808 at Neuss 30.01.92 with the 1517 Bergisch Gladbach - Wuppertal Vohwinkel. (S. McNally)

▼ Class 470/870 3-car emus stabled at Hamburg Altona 24.02.90 (D. Rowland)

```
420 420  421 420  420 920  TP
420 421  421 421  420 921  TP
420 422  421 422  420 922  TP
420 423  421 423  420 923  TP
420 424  421 424  420 924  TP
```

CLASSES 470/870   3-CAR UNITS

Built: 1959-70 by MAN/Wegmann.
System: 1200 V dc side contact third rail.
Electrical Equipment: BBC/Siemens.
Continuous Rating: 640 kW per power car.
Wheel Arrangements: Bo-Bo + 2-2 + Bo-Bo.
Weights: 42 + 27 + 42 tonnes.
Length: 22.280 + 20.960 + 22.280 m.
Maximum Speed: 80 km/h.
Seats: 63S + 66F + 63S.

```
470 101  870 101  470 401  AOP        470 124  870 124  470 424  AOP
470 102  870 102  470 402  AOP        470 125  870 125  470 425  AOP
470 103  870 103  470 403  AOP        470 126  870 126  470 426  AOP
470 104  870 104  470 404  AOP        470 127  870 127  470 427  AOP
470 105  870 105  470 405  AOP        470 128  870 128  470 428  AOP
470 106  870 106  470 406  AOP        470 129  870 129  470 429  AOP
470 107  870 107  470 407  AOP        470 130  870 130  470 430  AOP
470 108  870 108  470 408  AOP        470 131  870 131  470 431  AOP
470 109  870 109  470 409  AOP        470 132  870 132  470 432  AOP
470 110  870 110  470 410  AOP        470 133  870 133  470 433  AOP
470 111  870 111  470 411  AOP        470 134  870 134  470 434  AOP
470 112  870 112  470 412  AOP        470 135  870 135  470 435  AOP
470 113  870 113  470 413  AOP        470 136  870 136  470 436  AOP
470 114  870 114  470 414  AOP        470 137  870 137  470 437  AOP
470 115  870 115  470 415  AOP        470 138  870 138  470 438  AOP
470 116  870 116  470 416  AOP        470 139  870 139  470 439  AOP
470 117  870 117  470 417  AOP        470 140  870 140  470 440  AOP
470 118  870 118  470 418  AOP        470 141  870 141  470 441  AOP
470 119  870 119  470 419  AOP        470 142  870 142  470 442  AOP
470 120  870 120  470 420  AOP        470 143  870 143  470 443  AOP
470 121  870 121  470 421  AOP        470 144  870 144  470 444  AOP
470 122  870 122  470 422  AOP        470 145  870 145  470 445  AOP
470 123  870 123  470 423  AOP
```

CLASSES 471/871   3-CAR UNITS

Built: 1939-58 by MAN/LHW/Wegmann.
System: 1200 V dc side contact third rail.
Electrical Equipment: BBC.
Continuous Rating: 580 kW per power car.
Wheel Arrangements: Bo-Bo + 2-2 + Bo-Bo.
Weights: 50 + 31.2 + 50 tonnes.
Length: 21.280 + 19.960 + 21.280 m.
Maximum Speed: 80 km/h.
Seats: 66S + 68F + 66S.
Notes: A number of cars have changed identities over the years, due to withdrawals etc. Known changes are as follows: 471 101 was 471 441 until 01.01.81; 471 486 was 471 179 until 01.05.91; 871 014 was originally 871 025 until 01.01.86, then became 871 079 until 01.01.87 and 871 044 until 01.01.90.

471 101	871 101	471 401	AOP	471 138	871 138	471 438	AOP
471 102	871 102	471 402	AOP	471 140	871 140	471 440	AOP
471 104	871 104	471 404	AOP	471 142	871 142	471 442	AOP
471 105	871 105	471 405	AOP	471 143	871 143	471 443	AOP
471 106	871 106	471 406	AOP	471 151	871 151	471 451	AOP
471 107	871 107	471 407	AOP	471 152	871 152	471 452	AOP
471 109	871 109	471 409	AOP	471 161	871 161	471 461	AOP
471 110	871 110	471 410	AOP	471 162	871 162	471 462	AOP
471 111	871 111	471 411	AOP	471 163	871 163	471 463	AOP
471 112	871 112	471 412	AOP	471 164	871 164	471 464	AOP
471 113	871 113	471 413	AOP	471 165	871 165	471 465	AOP
471 114	871 114	471 414	AOP	471 166	871 166	471 466	AOP
471 115	871 115	471 415	AOP	471 167	871 167	471 467	AOP
471 116	871 116	471 416	AOP	471 168	871 168	471 468	AOP
471 117	871 117	471 417	AOP	471 169	871 169	471 469	AOP
471 118	871 118	471 418	AOP	471 170	871 170	471 470	AOP
471 120	871 120	471 420	AOP	471 171	871 171	471 471	AOP
471 121	871 121	471 421	AOP	471 172	871 172	471 472	AOP
471 122	871 122	471 422	AOP	471 173	871 173	471 473	AOP
471 123	871 123	471 423	AOP	471 174	871 174	471 474	AOP
471 124	871 124	471 424	AOP	471 175	871 175	471 475	AOP
471 126	871 126	471 426	AOP	471 176	871 176	471 476	AOP
471 127	871 127	471 427	AOP	471 177	871 177	471 477	AOP
471 128	871 128	471 428	AOP	471 178	871 178	471 478	AOP
471 129	871 129	471 429	AOP	471 180	871 180	471 480	AOP
471 130	871 130	471 430	AOP	471 181	871 181	471 481	AOP
471 131	871 131	471 431	AOP	471 182	871 182	471 482	AOP
471 132	871 132	471 432	AOP	471 183	871 183	471 483	AOP
471 134	871 134	471 434	AOP	471 184	871 184	471 484	AOP
471 135	871 135	471 435	AOP	471 185	871 185	471 485	AOP
471 137	871 137	471 437	AOP	471 186	871 186	471 486	AOP

Built: 1974-84 by LHW/MBB.
System: 1200 V dc side contact third rail.
Electrical Equipment: BBC/Siemens.
Continuous Rating: 500 kW per power car.
Wheel Arrangements: Bo-Bo + Bo-Bo + Bo-Bo.
Weights: 40 + 34 + 40 tonnes.
Length: 65.820 m.
Maximum Speed: 100 km/h.
Seats: 65S + 66F + 65S.

472 001	473 001	472 501	AOP	Alster
472 002	473 002	472 502	AOP	
472 003	473 003	472 503	AOP	
472 004	473 004	472 504	AOP	
472 005	473 005	472 505	AOP	
472 006	473 006	472 506	AOP	
472 007	473 007	472 507	AOP	
472 008	473 008	472 508	AOP	
472 009	473 009	472 509	AOP	
472 010	473 010	472 510	AOP	
472 011	473 011	472 511	AOP	
472 012	473 012	472 512	AOP	
472 013	473 013	472 513	AOP	
472 014	473 014	472 514	AOP	
472 015	473 015	472 515	AOP	
472 016	473 016	472 516	AOP	
472 017	473 017	472 517	AOP	
472 018	473 018	472 518	AOP	
472 019	473 019	472 519	AOP	
472 020	473 020	472 520	AOP	
472 021	473 021	472 521	AOP	
472 022	473 022	472 522	AOP	
472 023	473 023	472 523	AOP	
472 024	473 024	472 524	AOP	
472 025	473 025	472 525	AOP	
472 026	473 026	472 526	AOP	
472 027	473 027	472 527	AOP	
472 028	473 028	472 528	AOP	
472 029	473 029	472 529	AOP	
472 030	473 030	472 530	AOP	Elbe
472 031	473 031	472 531	AOP	
472 032	473 032	472 532	AOP	
472 033	473 033	472 533	AOP	

▲ A Class 472/3 3-car emu approaches Hamburg Altona 24.02.90   (D. Rowland)

▼ 275 763 + 275 764 (new nos. 475 119 + 875 119) at Berlin Schöneweide 12.04.91
(D. Rowland)

472 034	473 034	472 534	AOP	
472 035	473 035	472 535	AOP	
472 036	473 036	472 536	AOP	
472 037	473 037	472 537	AOP	
472 038	473 038	472 538	AOP	
472 039	473 039	472 539	AOP	
472 040	473 040	472 540	AOP	
472 041	473 041	472 541	AOP	
472 042	473 042	472 542	AOP	
472 043	473 043	472 543	AOP	
472 044	473 044	472 544	AOP	
472 045	473 045	472 545	AOP	Harburg
472 046	473 046	472 546	AOP	
472 047	473 047	472 547	AOP	
472 048	473 048	472 548	AOP	
472 049	473 049	472 549	AOP	
472 050	473 050	472 550	AOP	
472 051	473 051	472 551	AOP	
472 052	473 052	472 552	AOP	
472 053	473 053	472 553	AOP	
472 054	473 054	472 554	AOP	
472 055	473 055	472 555	AOP	
472 056	473 056	472 556	AOP	
472 057	473 057	472 557	AOP	
472 058	473 058	472 558	AOP	
472 059	473 059	472 559	AOP	
472 060	473 060	472 560	AOP	
472 061	473 061	472 561	AOP	Suderelbe
472 062	473 062	472 562	AOP	

CLASSES 475/875   2-CAR HALF UNITS

Built: 1927-30 by AEG/Siemens/BEW. Refurbished 1986 onwards by Waggon Union.
System: 800 V dc third rail.
Electrical Equipment: AEG/Siemens/BEW.
Continuous Rating: 440 kW.
Wheel Arrangements: Bo-Bo + 2-2.
Weight: 65.60 tonnes.
Length: 35.460 m.
Maximum Speed: 80 km/h.
Seats: 115-127.
Note: Power and trailer cars are coupled in pairs. Four pairs are coupled together to form
the normal train formation.

475 001 (275 003)	875 001 (275 004)	BBW
475 002 (275 021)	875 002 (275 022)	BBW
475 003 (275 031)	875 003 (275 032)	BBW
475 004 (275 037)	875 004 (275 038)	BBW
475 005 (275 045)	875 005 (275 046)	BBW
475 006 (275 053)	875 006 (275 054)	BBW
475 007 (275 059)	875 007 (275 060)	BBW
475 008 (275 061)	875 008 (275 062)	BBW
475 009 (275 081)	875 009 (275 082)	BBW
475 010 (275 083)	875 010 (275 084)	BBW
475 011 (275 085)	875 011 (275 086)	BBW
475 012 (275 095)	875 012 (275 096)	BBW
475 013 (275 109)	875 013 (275 110)	BBW
475 014 (275 115)	875 014 (275 116)	BBW
475 015 (275 137)	875 015 (275 138)	BBW
475 016 (275 155)	875 016 (275 156)	BBW
475 017 (275 169)	875 017 (275 170)	BBW
475 018 (275 171)	875 018 (275 172)	BBW
475 019 (275 199)	875 019 (275 200)	BBW
475 020 (275 223)	875 020 (275 224)	BBW
475 021 (275 227)	875 021 (275 228)	BBW
475 022 (275 233)	875 022 (275 234)	BBW
475 023 (275 245)	875 023 (275 246)	BBW
475 024 (275 247)	875 024 (275 248)	BBW
475 025 (275 251)	875 025 (275 252)	BBW
475 026 (275 255)	875 026 (275 256)	BBW
475 027 (275 257)	875 027 (275 258)	BBW
475 028 (275 265)	875 028 (275 266)	BBW
475 029 (275 289)	875 029 (275 290)	BBW
475 030 (275 311)	875 030 (275 312)	BBW
475 031 (275 313)	875 031 (275 314)	BBW
475 032 (275 315)	875 032 (275 316)	BBW
475 033 (275 317)	875 033 (275 318)	BBW
475 034 (275 333)	875 034 (275 334)	BBW
475 035 (275 335)	875 035 (275 336)	BBW
475 036 (275 339)	875 036 (275 340)	BBW
475 037 (275 343)	875 037 (275 344)	BBW
475 038 (275 351)	875 038 (275 352)	BBW
475 039 (275 355)	875 039 (275 356)	BBW
475 040 (275 357)	875 040 (275 358)	BBW
475 041 (275 363)	875 041 (275 364)	BBW
475 042 (275 365)	875 042 (275 366)	BBW
475 043 (275 377)	875 043 (275 378)	BBW
475 044 (275 381)	875 044 (275 382)	BBW

475 045 (275 385)	875 045 (275 386)	BBW
475 046 (275 387)	875 046 (275 388)	BBW
475 047 (275 391)	875 047 (275 392)	BBW
475 048 (275 397)	875 048 (275 398)	BBW
475 049 (275 407)	875 049 (275 408)	BBW
475 050 (275 411)	875 050 (275 412)	BBW
475 051 (275 413)	875 051 (275 414)	BBW
475 052 (275 415)	875 052 (275 416)	BBW
475 053 (275 417)	875 053 (275 418)	BBW
475 054 (275 419)	875 054 (275 420)	BBW
475 055 (275 421)	875 055 (275 422)	BBW
475 056 (275 425)	875 056 (275 426)	BBF
475 057 (275 429)	875 057 (275 430)	BBW
475 058 (275 431)	875 058 (275 432)	BBW
475 059 (275 433)	875 059 (275 434)	BBF
475 060 (275 435)	875 060 (275 436)	BBW
475 061 (275 449)	875 061 (275 450)	BBW
475 062 (275 459)	875 062 (275 460)	BBW
475 063 (275 461)	875 063 (275 462)	BBF
475 064 (275 467)	875 064 (275 468)	BBF
475 065 (275 475)	875 065 (275 476)	BBW
475 066 (275 479)	875 066 (275 480)	BBF
475 067 (275 487)	875 067 (275 488)	BBW
475 068 (275 491)	875 068 (275 492)	BBW
475 069 (275 495)	875 069 (275 496)	BBW
475 070 (275 499)	875 070 (275 500)	BBF
475 071 (275 501)	875 071 (275 502)	BBW
475 072 (275 503)	875 072 (275 504)	BBF
475 073 (275 505)	875 073 (275 506)	BBW
475 074 (275 511)	875 074 (275 512)	BBF
475 075 (275 517)	875 075 (275 518)	BBW
475 076 (275 519)	875 076 (275 520)	BBW
475 077 (275 521)	875 077 (275 522)	BBW
475 078 (275 525)	875 078 (275 526)	BBW
475 079 (275 531)	875 079 (275 532)	BBW
475 080 (275 533)	875 080 (275 534)	BBW
475 081 (275 535)	875 081 (275 536)	BBW
475 082 (275 539)	875 082 (275 540)	BBW
475 083 (275 541)	875 083 (275 542)	BBW
475 084 (275 543)	875 084 (275 544)	BBW
475 085 (275 551)	875 085 (275 552)	BBW
475 086 (275 557)	875 086 (275 558)	BBW
475 087 (275 559)	875 087 (275 560)	BBW
475 088 (275 561)	875 088 (275 562)	BBW

475 089 (275 563)	875 089 (275 564)	BBW
475 090 (275 565)	875 090 (275 566)	BBW
475 091 (275 573)	875 091 (275 574)	BBW
475 092 (275 581)	875 092 (275 582)	BBF
475 093 (275 583)	875 093 (275 584)	BBW
475 094 (275 587)	875 094 (275 588)	BBW
475 095 (275 589)	875 095 (275 590)	BBW
475 096 (275 591)	875 096 (275 592)	BBW
475 097 (275 593)	875 097 (275 594)	BBW
475 098 (275 595)	875 098 (275 596)	BBF
475 099 (275 597)	875 099 (275 598)	BBW
475 100 (275 599)	875 100 (275 600)	BBW
475 101 (275 601)	875 101 (275 602)	BBW
475 102 (275 603)	875 102 (275 604)	BBF
475 103 (275 605)	875 103 (275 606)	BBW
475 104 (275 609)	875 104 (275 610)	BBF
475 105 (275 619)	875 105 (275 620)	BBF
475 106 (275 621)	875 106 (275 622)	BBF
475 107 (275 623)	875 107 (275 624)	BBF
475 108 (275 631)	875 108 (275 632)	BBF
475 109 (275 637)	875 109 (275 638)	BBF
475 110 (275 663)	875 110 (275 664)	BBF
475 111 (275 667)	875 111 (275 668)	BBF
475 112 (275 697)	875 112 (275 698)	BBF
475 113 (275 703)	875 113 (275 704)	BBF
475 114 (275 711)	875 114 (275 712)	BBF
475 115 (275 741)	875 115 (275 742)	BBF
475 116 (275 743)	875 116 (275 744)	BBF
475 117 (275 745)	875 117 (275 746)	BBF
475 118 (275 761)	875 118 (275 762)	BBF
475 119 (275 763)	875 119 (275 764)	BBF
475 120 (275 765)	875 120 (275 766)	BBF
475 121 (275 779)	875 121 (275 780)	BBF
475 122 (275 797)	875 122 (275 798)	BBF
475 123 (275 809)	875 123 (275 810)	BBF
475 124 (275 833)	875 124 (275 834)	BBF
475 125 (275 953)	875 125 (275 954)	BBF
475 126 (275 959)	875 126 (275 960)	BBF
475 127 (275 967)	875 127 (275 968)	BBG
475 128 (275 971)	875 128 (275 972)	BBG
475 129 (275 327)	875 129 (275 328)	(ZR)
475 130 (275 347)	875 130 (275 348)	(ZR)
475 131 (275 375)	875 131 (275 376)	(ZR)
475 132 (275 403)	875 132 (275 404)	(ZR)

475 133 (275 427)	875 133 (275 428)	(ZR)
475 134 (275 453)	875 134 (275 454)	(ZR)
475 135 (275 469)	875 135 (275 470)	(ZR)
475 136 (275 483)	875 136 (275 484)	(ZR)
475 137 (275 507)	875 137 (275 508)	(ZR)
475 138 (275 529)	875 138 (275 530)	(ZR)
475 139 (275 545)	875 139 (275 546)	(ZR)
475 140 (275 611)	875 140 (275 612)	(ZR)
475 141 (275 629)	875 141 (275 630)	(ZR)
475 142 (275 639)	875 142 (275 640)	(ZR)
475 143 (275 647)	875 143 (275 648)	(ZR)
475 144 (275 649)	875 144 (275 650)	(ZR)
475 145 (275 655)	875 145 (275 656)	(Z)
475 146 (275 665)	875 146 (275 666)	(ZR)
475 147 (275 687)	875 147 (275 688)	(ZR)
475 148 (275 705)	875 148 (275 706)	(ZR)
475 149 (275 707)	875 149 (275 708)	(ZR)
475 150 (275 721)	875 150 (275 722)	(ZR)
475 151 (275 685)	875 151 (275 686)	(Z)
475 152 (275 805)	875 152 (275 806)	(Z)
475 153 (275 831)	875 153 (275 832)	(ZR)
475 154 (275 947)	875 154 (275 948)	(ZR)
475 155 (275 951)	875 155 (275 952)	(ZR)
475 156 (275 955)	875 156 (275 956)	(ZR)
475 157 (275 963)	875 157 (275 964)	(ZR)
475 158 (275 965)	875 158 (275 966)	(ZR)
475 159 (275 493)	875 159 (275 494)	BBG
475 160 (275 961)	875 160 (275 962)	BBG
475 163 (275 733)		(Z)
475 601 (275 319)	875 601 (275 320)	BBW
475 602 (275 353)	875 602 (275 354)	BBW
475 603 (275 513)	875 603 (275 514)	BBW
475 604 (275 633)	875 604 (275 634)	BBW
475 605 (275 641)	875 605 (275 642)	BBW
475 606 (275 651)	875 606 (275 652)	BBW
475 607 (275 675)	875 607 (275 676)	BBW
475 608 (275 683)	875 608 (275 684)	BBW
475 609 (275 767)	875 609 (275 768)	BBW
475 610 (275 695)	875 610 (275 696)	BBW
475 611 (275 699)	875 611 (275 700)	BBW
475 612 (275 701)	875 612 (275 702)	BBW
475 613 (275 719)	875 613 (275 720)	BBW
475 614 (275 729)	875 614 (275 730)	BBW
475 615 (275 735)	875 615 (275 736)	BBW

CLASSES 476/876   2-CAR HALF UNITS

Built: 1936-50 by O & K/Dessau/Wegmann. Rebuilt at DR Schöneweide works.
System: 800 V dc third rail.
Electrical Equipment: AEG/Siemens.
Continuous Rating: 440 kW.
Wheel Arrangements: Bo-Bo + 2-2.
Weight: 76 tonnes.
Length: 35.560 m.
Maximum Speed: 80 km/h.
Seats: 115.
Note: Power and trailer cars are coupled in pairs. Four pairs are coupled together to form the normal train formation.

476 001 (276 509)	876 001 (276 510)	BBF
476 002 (276 513)	876 002 (276 514)	BBF
476 003 (276 515)	876 003 (276 516)	BBF
476 004 (276 517)	876 004 (276 518)	BBF
476 005 (276 519)	876 005 (276 520)	BBF
476 006 (276 521)	876 006 (276 522)	BBF
476 007 (276 523)	876 007 (276 524)	BBF
476 008 (276 525)	876 008 (276 526)	BBF
476 009 (276 527)	876 009 (276 528)	BBF
476 010 (276 529)	876 010 (276 530)	BBF
476 011 (276 531)	876 011 (276 532)	BBF
476 012 (276 533)	876 012 (276 534)	BBF
476 013 (276 535)	876 013 (276 536)	BBF
476 014 (276 537)	876 014 (276 538)	BBF
476 015 (276 539)	876 015 (276 540)	BBF
476 016 (276 541)	876 016 (276 542)	BBF
476 017 (276 543)	876 017 (276 544)	BBF
476 018 (276 545)	876 018 (276 546)	BBF
476 019 (276 547)	876 019 (276 548)	BBF
476 020 (276 549)	876 020 (276 550)	BBF
476 021 (276 551)	876 021 (276 552)	BBF
476 022 (276 553)	876 022 (276 554)	BBF
476 023 (276 555)	876 023 (276 556)	BBF
476 024 (276 557)	876 024 (276 558)	BBF
476 025 (276 559)	876 025 (276 560)	BBF
476 026 (276 561)	876 026 (276 562)	BBF
476 027 (276 563)	876 027 (276 564)	BBF
476 028 (276 565)	876 028 (276 566)	BBF
476 029 (276 567)	876 029 (276 568)	BBF
476 030 (276 569)	876 030 (276 570)	BBF
476 031 (276 507)	876 031 (276 508)	BBF

476 032 (276 511)	876 032 (276 512)	BBF
476 301 (276 119)	876 301 (276 120)	BBF
476 302 (276 137)	876 302 (276 138)	BBF
476 303 (276 139)	876 303 (276 140)	BBF
476 304 (276 141)	876 304 (276 142)	BBF
476 305 (276 143)	876 305 (276 144)	BBF
476 306 (276 151)	876 306 (276 152)	BBF
476 307 (276 153)	876 307 (276 154)	BBF
476 308 (276 155)	876 308 (276 156)	BBF
476 309 (276 157)	876 309 (276 158)	BBF
476 310 (276 159)	876 310 (276 160)	BBF
476 311 (276 163)	876 311 (276 164)	BBF
476 312 (276 165)	876 312 (276 166)	BBF
476 313 (276 167)	876 313 (276 168)	BBF
476 314 (276 169)	876 314 (276 170)	BBF
476 315 (276 171)	876 315 (276 172)	BBF
476 316 (276 173)	876 316 (276 174)	BBF
476 317 (276 175)	876 317 (276 176)	BBF
476 318 (276 177)	876 318 (276 178)	BBF
476 319 (276 181)	876 319 (276 182)	BBF
476 320 (276 183)	876 320 (276 184)	BBF
476 321 (276 185)	876 321 (276 186)	BBF
476 322 (276 189)	876 322 (276 190)	BBF
476 323 (276 191)	876 323 (276 192)	BBF
476 324 (276 193)	876 324 (276 194)	BBF
476 325 (276 195)	876 325 (276 196)	BBF
476 326 (276 197)	876 326 (276 198)	BBF
476 327 (276 199)	876 327 (276 200)	BBF
476 328 (276 201)	876 328 (276 202)	BBF
476 329 (276 203)	876 329 (276 204)	BBF
476 330 (276 207)	876 330 (276 208)	BBF
476 331 (276 219)	876 331 (276 220)	BBF
476 332 (276 223)	876 332 (276 224)	BBF
476 333 (276 227)	876 333 (276 228)	BBF
476 334 (276 229)	876 334 (276 230)	BBF
476 335 (276 231)	876 335 (276 232)	BBF
476 336 (276 233)	876 336 (276 234)	BBF
476 337 (276 235)	876 337 (276 236)	BBF
476 338 (276 239)	876 338 (276 240)	BBF
476 339 (276 241)	876 339 (276 242)	BBF
476 340 (276 251)	876 340 (276 252)	BBF
476 341 (276 253)	876 341 (276 254)	BBF
476 342 (276 267)	876 342 (276 268)	BBF
476 343 (276 277)	876 343 (276 278)	BBF

476 344 (276 279)	876 344 (276 280)	BBF
476 345 (276 283)	876 345 (276 284)	BBF
476 346 (276 285)	876 346 (276 286)	BBF
476 347 (276 287)	876 347 (276 288)	BBF
476 348 (276 289)	876 348 (276 290)	BBF
476 349 (276 291)	876 349 (276 292)	BBF
476 350 (276 293)	876 350 (276 294)	BBF
476 351 (276 299)	876 351 (276 300)	BBF
476 352 (276 301)	876 352 (276 302)	BBF
476 353 (276 303)	876 353 (276 304)	BBF
476 354 (276 305)	876 354 (276 306)	BBF
476 355 (276 307)	876 355 (276 308)	BBF
476 356 (276 311)	876 356 (276 312)	BBF
476 357 (276 313)	876 357 (276 314)	BBF
476 358 (276 317)	876 358 (276 318)	BBF
476 359 (276 319)	876 359 (276 320)	BBF
476 360 (276 323)	876 360 (276 324)	BBF
476 361 (276 325)	876 361 (276 326)	BBF
476 362 (276 327)	876 362 (276 328)	BBF
476 363 (276 329)	876 363 (276 330)	BBF
476 364 (276 331)	876 364 (276 332)	BBF
476 365 (276 333)	876 365 (276 334)	BBF
476 366 (276 335)	876 366 (276 336)	BBF
476 367 (276 337)	876 367 (276 338)	BBF
476 368 (276 339)	876 368 (276 340)	BBF
476 369 (276 341)	876 369 (276 342)	BBF
476 370 (276 343)	876 370 (276 344)	BBF
476 371 (276 345)	876 371 (276 346)	BBF
476 372 (276 347)	876 372 (276 348)	BBF
476 373 (276 349)	876 373 (276 350)	BBF
476 374 (276 353)	876 374 (276 354)	BBF
476 375 (276 357)	876 375 (276 358)	BBF
476 376 (276 359)	876 376 (276 360)	BBF
476 377 (276 363)	876 377 (276 364)	BBF
476 378 (276 369)	876 378 (276 370)	BBF
476 379 (276 371)	876 379 (276 372)	BBF
476 380 (276 375)	876 380 (276 376)	BBF
476 381 (276 377)	876 381 (276 378)	BBF
476 382 (276 379)	876 382 (276 380)	BBF
476 383 (276 383)	876 383 (276 384)	BBF
476 384 (276 385)	876 384 (276 386)	BBF
476 385 (276 387)	876 385 (276 388)	BBF
476 386 (276 391)	876 386 (276 392)	BBF
476 387 (276 395)	876 387 (276 396)	BBF

476 388 (276 397)	876 388 (276 398)	BBF
476 389 (276 399)	876 389 (276 400)	BBF
476 390 (276 401)	876 390 (276 402)	BBF
476 391 (276 403)	876 391 (276 404)	BBF
476 392 (276 405)	876 392 (276 406)	BBF
476 393 (276 407)	876 393 (276 408)	BBF
476 394 (276 409)	876 394 (276 410)	BBF
476 395 (276 411)	876 395 (276 412)	BBF
476 396 (276 415)	876 396 (276 416)	BBF
476 397 (276 417)	876 397 (276 418)	BBF
476 398 (276 419)	876 398 (276 420)	BBF
476 399 (276 421)	876 399 (276 422)	BBF
476 400 (276 423)	876 400 (276 424)	BBF
476 401 (276 425)	876 401 (276 426)	BBF
476 402 (276 429)	876 402 (276 430)	BBF
476 403 (276 431)	876 403 (276 432)	BBF
476 404 (276 433)	876 404 (276 434)	BBF
476 405 (276 435)	876 405 (276 436)	BBF
476 406 (276 437)	876 406 (276 438)	BBF
476 407 (276 439)	876 407 (276 440)	BBF
476 408 (276 441)	876 408 (276 442)	BBF
476 409 (276 443)	876 409 (276 444)	BBF
476 410 (276 445)	876 410 (276 446)	BBF
476 411 (276 449)	876 411 (276 450)	BBF
476 412 (276 451)	876 412 (276 452)	BBF
476 413 (276 453)	876 413 (276 454)	BBF
476 414 (276 457)	876 414 (276 458)	BBF
476 415 (276 463)	876 415 (276 464)	BBF
476 416 (276 465)	876 416 (276 466)	BBF
476 417 (276 467)	876 417 (276 468)	BBF
476 418 (276 469)	876 418 (276 470)	BBF
476 419 (276 471)	876 419 (276 472)	BBF
476 420 (276 473)	876 420 (276 474)	BBF
476 421 (276 475)	876 421 (276 476)	BBF
476 422 (276 477)	876 422 (276 478)	BBF
476 423 (276 481)	876 423 (276 482)	BBF
476 424 (276 483)	876 424 (276 484)	BBF
476 425 (276 485)	876 425 (276 486)	BBF
476 426 (276 487)	876 426 (276 488)	BBF
476 427 (276 489)	876 427 (276 490)	BBF
476 428 (276 491)	876 428 (276 492)	BBF
476 429 (276 497)	876 429 (276 498)	BBF
476 430 (276 499)	876 430 (276 500)	BBF
476 431 (276 501)	876 431 (276 502)	BBF

476 432 (276 503)	876 432 (276 504)	BBF
476 433 (276 505)	876 433 (276 506)	BBF
476 434 (276 111)	876 434 (276 112)	BBF
476 435 (276 113)	876 435 (276 114)	BBF
476 436 (276 115)	876 436 (276 116)	BBF
476 437 (276 117)	876 437 (276 118)	BBF
476 438 (276 123)	876 438 (276 124)	BBF
476 439 (276 129)	876 439 (276 130)	BBF
476 440 (276 131)	876 440 (276 132)	BBF
476 441 (276 145)	876 441 (276 146)	BBF
476 442 (276 147)	876 442 (276 148)	BBF
476 443 (276 149)	876 443 (276 150)	BBF
476 444 (276 179)	876 444 (276 180)	BBF
476 445 (276 214)	876 445 (276 214)	BBF
476 446 (276 217)	876 446 (276 218)	BBF
476 447 (276 221)	876 447 (276 222)	BBF
476 448 (276 257)	876 448 (276 258)	BBF
476 449 (276 261)	876 449 (276 262)	BBF
476 450 (276 263)	876 450 (276 264)	BBF
476 451 (276 265)	876 451 (276 266)	BBF
476 452 (276 271)	876 452 (276 272)	BBF
476 453 (276 273)	876 453 (276 274)	BBF
476 454 (276 275)	876 454 (276 276)	BBF
476 455 (276 281)	876 455 (276 282)	BBF
476 456 (276 295)	876 456 (276 296)	BBF
476 457 (276 297)	876 457 (276 298)	BBF
476 458 (276 309)	876 458 (276 310)	BBF
476 459 (276 381)	876 459 (276 382)	BBF
476 460 (276 427)	876 460 (276 428)	BBF
476 461 (276 455)	876 461 (276 456)	BBF
476 462 (276 459)	876 462 (276 460)	BBF
476 463 (276 479)	876 463 (276 480)	BBF
476 464 (276 493)	876 464 (276 494)	BBF
476 465 (276 495)	876 465 (276 496)	BBF
476 466 (276 205)	876 466 (276 206)	BBF
476 467 (276 243)	876 467 (276 244)	BBF
476 468 (276 245)	876 468 (276 246)	BBF
476 469 (276 255)	876 469 (276 256)	BBF
476 470 (276 269)	876 470 (276 270)	BBF
476 471 (276 321)	876 471 (276 322)	BBF
476 472 (276 355)	876 472 (276 356)	BBF
476 473 (276 361)	876 473 (276 362)	BBF
476 474 (276 365)	876 474 (276 366)	BBF
476 475 (276 367)	876 475 (276 368)	BBF

476 476 (276 373)	876 476 (276 374)	BBF
476 477 (276 389)	876 477 (276 390)	BBF
476 478 (276 413)	876 478 (276 414)	BBF
476 479 (276 447)	876 479 (276 448)	BBF
476 480 (276 461)	876 480 (276 462)	BBF
476 601 (277 069)	876 601 (277 070)	(Z)
476 602 (276 075)	876 602 (276 076)	(Z)

CLASSES 477/877   2-CAR HALF UNITS

Built: 1937-45 by O & K/Dessau/Wegmann.
System: 800 V dc third rail.
Electrical Equipment: AEG/Siemens.
Continuous Rating:
Wheel Arrangements: Bo-Bo + 2-2
Weight: 67.4 tonnes.
Length: 35.560 m.
Maximum Speed: 80 km/h.
Seats: 119.
Note: Power and trailer cars are coupled in pairs. Four pairs are coupled together to form the normal train formation.

477 001 (277 001)	877 001 (277 002)	BBG
477 002 (277 005)	877 002 (277 006)	BBG
477 003 (277 007)	877 003 (277 008)	BBG
477 004 (277 009)	877 004 (277 010)	BBG
477 005 (277 011)	877 005 (277 012)	BBG
477 006 (277 013)	877 006 (277 014)	BBG
477 007 (277 015)	877 007 (277 016)	BBG
477 008 (277 017)	877 008 (277 018)	BBG
477 009 (277 019)	877 009 (277 020)	BBG
477 010 (277 021)	877 010 (277 022)	BBG
477 011 (277 023)	877 011 (277 024)	BBG
477 012 (277 025)	877 012 (277 026)	BBG
477 013 (277 029)	877 013 (277 030)	BBG
477 014 (277 031)	877 014 (277 032)	BBG
477 015 (277 035)	877 015 (277 034)	BBG
477 016 (277 037)	877 016 (277 038)	BBG
477 017 (277 039)	877 017 (277 040)	BBG
477 018 (277 041)	877 018 (277 042)	BBG
477 019 (277 045)	877 019 (277 046)	BBG
477 020 (277 049)	877 020 (277 050)	BBG
477 021 (277 053)	877 021 (277 054)	BBG

▲ 277 297 + 277 298 (new nos. 477 133 + 877 133) at Berlin Schöneweide 12.04.91
(D. Rowland)

▼ The unique Class 491 unit at Würzburg 29.05.88 (D.J. Glossop).

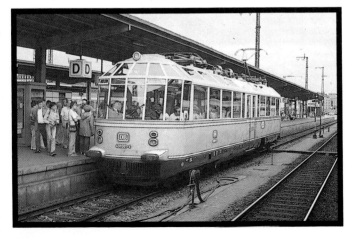

477 022 (277 055)	877 022 (277 056)	BBG
477 023 (277 057)	877 023 (277 058)	BBG
477 024 (277 059)	877 024 (277 060)	BBG
477 025 (277 061)	877 025 (277 062)	BBG
477 026 (277 067)	877 026 (277 068)	BBG
477 027 (277 071)	877 027 (277 072)	BBG
477 028 (277 075)	877 028 (277 076)	BBG
477 029 (277 077)	877 029 (277 078)	BBG
477 030 (277 079)	877 030 (277 080)	BBG
477 031 (277 081)	877 031 (277 082)	BBG
477 032 (277 083)	877 032 (277 084)	BBG
477 033 (277 085)	877 033 (277 086)	BBG
477 034 (277 089)	877 034 (277 090)	BBG
477 035 (277 091)	877 035 (277 092)	BBG
477 036 (277 093)	877 036 (277 094)	BBG
477 037 (277 095)	877 037 (277 096)	BBG
477 038 (277 097)	877 038 (277 098)	BBG
477 039 (277 099)	877 039 (277 100)	BBG
477 040 (277 101)	877 040 (277 102)	BBG
477 041 (277 105)	877 041 (277 106)	BBG
477 042 (277 107)	877 042 (277 108)	BBG
477 043 (277 109)	877 043 (277 110)	BBG
477 044 (277 111)	877 044 (277 112)	BBG
477 045 (277 113)	877 045 (277 114)	BBG
477 046 (277 115)	877 046 (277 116)	BBG
477 047 (277 117)	877 047 (277 118)	BBG
477 048 (277 119)	877 048 (277 120)	BBG
477 049 (277 121)	877 049 (277 122)	BBG
477 050 (277 123)	877 050 (277 124)	BBG
477 051 (277 125)	877 051 (277 126)	BBG
477 052 (277 127)	877 052 (277 128)	BBG
477 053 (277 129)	877 053 (277 130)	BBG
477 054 (277 131)	877 054 (277 132)	BBG
477 055 (277 133)	877 055 (277 134)	BBG
477 056 (277 135)	877 056 (277 136)	BBG
477 057 (277 137)	877 057 (277 138)	BBG
477 058 (277 139)	877 058 (277 140)	BBG
477 059 (277 141)	877 059 (277 142)	BBG
477 060 (277 143)	877 060 (277 144)	BBG
477 061 (277 145)	877 061 (277 146)	BBG
477 062 (277 147)	877 062 (277 148)	BBG
477 063 (277 149)	877 063 (277 150)	BBG
477 064 (277 151)	877 064 (277 152)	BBG
477 065 (277 153)	877 065 (277 154)	BBG
477 066 (277 155)	877 066 (277 156)	BBG

477 067 (277 157)	877 067 (277 158)	BBG
477 068 (277 159)	877 068 (277 160)	BBG
477 069 (277 161)	877 069 (277 162)	BBG
477 070 (277 163)	877 070 (277 164)	BBG
477 071 (277 167)	877 071 (277 168)	BBG
477 072 (277 169)	877 072 (277 170)	BBG
477 073 (277 171)	877 073 (277 172)	BBG
477 074 (277 173)	877 074 (277 174)	BBG
477 075 (277 175)	877 075 (277 176)	BBG
477 076 (277 177)	877 076 (277 178)	BBG
477 077 (277 179)	877 077 (277 180)	BBG
477 078 (277 181)	877 078 (277 182)	BBG
477 079 (277 183)	877 079 (277 184)	BBG
477 080 (277 185)	877 080 (277 186)	BBG
477 081 (277 187)	877 081 (277 188)	BBG
477 082 (277 189)	877 082 (277 190)	BBG
477 083 (277 191)	877 083 (277 192)	BBG
477 084 (277 193)	877 084 (277 194)	BBG
477 085 (277 195)	877 085 (277 196)	BBG
477 086 (277 197)	877 086 (277 198)	BBG
477 087 (277 199)	877 087 (277 200)	BBG
477 088 (277 203)	877 088 (277 204)	BBG
477 089 (277 205)	877 089 (277 206)	BBG
477 090 (277 207)	877 090 (277 208)	BBG
477 091 (277 209)	877 091 (277 210)	BBG
477 092 (277 211)	877 092 (277 212)	BBG
477 093 (277 213)	877 093 (277 214)	BBG
477 094 (277 215)	877 094 (277 216)	BBG
477 095 (277 217)	877 095 (277 218)	BBG
477 096 (277 219)	877 096 (277 220)	BBG
477 097 (277 223)	877 097 (277 224)	BBG
477 098 (277 225)	877 098 (277 226)	BBG
477 099 (277 227)	877 099 (277 228)	BBG
477 100 (277 229)	877 100 (277 230)	BBG
477 101 (277 231)	877 101 (277 232)	BBG
477 102 (277 233)	877 102 (277 234)	BBG
477 103 (277 235)	877 103 (277 236)	BBG
477 104 (277 237)	877 104 (277 238)	BBG
477 105 (277 239)	877 105 (277 240)	BBG
477 106 (277 241)	877 106 (277 242)	BBG
477 107 (277 243)	877 107 (277 244)	BBG
477 108 (277 245)	877 108 (277 246)	BBG
477 109 (277 247)	877 109 (277 248)	BBG
477 110 (277 249)	877 110 (277 250)	BBG
477 111 (277 251)	877 111 (277 252)	BBG

477 112 (277 253)	877 112 (277 254)	BBG
477 113 (277 255)	877 113 (277 256)	BBG
477 114 (277 257)	877 114 (277 258)	BBG
477 115 (277 259)	877 115 (277 260)	BBG
477 116 (277 261)	877 116 (277 262)	BBG
477 117 (277 263)	877 117 (277 264)	BBG
477 118 (277 265)	877 118 (277 266)	BBG
477 119 (277 267)	877 119 (277 268)	BBG
477 120 (277 269)	877 120 (277 270)	BBG
477 121 (277 271)	877 121 (277 272)	BBG
477 122 (277 273)	877 122 (277 274)	BBG
477 123 (277 275)	877 123 (277 276)	BBG
477 124 (277 277)	877 124 (277 278)	BBG
477 125 (277 279)	877 125 (277 280)	BBG
477 126 (277 281)	877 126 (277 282)	BBG
477 127 (277 285)	877 127 (277 286)	BBG
477 128 (277 287)	877 128 (277 288)	BBG
477 129 (277 289)	877 129 (277 290)	BBG
477 130 (277 291)	877 130 (277 292)	BBG
477 131 (277 293)	877 131 (277 294)	BBG
477 132 (277 295)	877 132 (277 296)	BBG
477 133 (277 297)	877 133 (277 298)	BBG
477 134 (277 299)	877 134 (277 300)	BBG
477 135 (277 301)	877 135 (277 302)	BBG
477 136 (277 303)	877 136 (277 304)	BBG
477 137 (277 305)	877 137 (277 306)	BBG
477 138 (277 307)	877 138 (277 308)	BBG
477 139 (277 309)	877 139 (277 310)	BBG
477 140 (277 311)	877 140 (277 312)	BBG
477 141 (277 313)	877 141 (277 314)	BBG
477 142 (277 315)	877 142 (277 316)	BBG
477 143 (277 317)	877 143 (277 318)	BBG
477 144 (277 319)	877 144 (277 320)	BBG
477 145 (277 321)	877 145 (277 322)	BBG
477 146 (277 323)	877 146 (277 324)	BBG
477 147 (277 325)	877 147 (277 326)	BBG
477 148 (277 327)	877 148 (277 328)	BBG
477 149 (277 329)	877 149 (277 330)	BBG
477 150 (277 331)	877 150 (277 332)	BBG
477 151 (277 333)	877 151 (277 334)	BBG
477 152 (277 335)	877 152 (277 336)	BBG
477 153 (277 337)	877 153 (277 338)	BBG
477 154 (277 339)	877 154 (277 340)	BBG
477 155 (277 341)	877 155 (277 342)	BBG
477 156 (277 343)	877 156 (277 344)	BBG

477 157 (277 345)	877 157 (277 346)	BBG
477 158 (277 347)	877 158 (277 348)	BBG
477 159 (277 349)	877 159 (277 350)	BBG
477 160 (277 351)	877 160 (277 352)	BBG
477 161 (277 353)	877 161 (277 354)	BBG
477 162 (277 355)	877 162 (277 356)	BBG
477 163 (277 357)	877 163 (277 358)	BBG
477 164 (277 359)	877 164 (277 360)	BBG
477 165 (277 361)	877 165 (277 362)	BBG
477 166 (277 363)	877 166 (277 364)	BBG
477 167 (277 365)	877 167 (277 366)	BBG
477 168 (277 367)	877 168 (277 368)	BBG
477 169 (277 369)	877 169 (277 370)	BBG
477 170 (277 371)	877 170 (277 372)	BBG
477 171 (277 373)	877 171 (277 374)	BBG
477 172 (277 375)	877 172 (277 376)	BBG
477 173 (277 377)	877 173 (277 378)	BBG
477 174 (277 379)	877 174 (277 380)	BBG
477 175 (277 385)	877 175 (277 384)	BBG
477 176 (277 387)	877 176 (277 388)	BBG
477 177 (277 389)	877 177 (277 390)	BBG
477 178 (277 393)	877 178 (277 394)	BBG
477 179 (277 397)	877 179 (277 398)	BBG
477 180 (277 399)	877 180 (277 400)	BBG
477 181 (277 401)	877 181 (277 402)	BBG
477 182 (277 423)	877 182 (277 424)	BBG
477 183 (277 425)	877 183 (277 426)	BBG
477 184 (277 427)	877 184 (277 428)	BBG
477 185 (277 429)	877 185 (277 430)	BBG
477 186 (277 433)	877 186 (277 434)	BBG
477 187 (277 435)	877 187 (277 436)	BBG
477 188 (277 437)	877 188 (277 438)	BBG
477 189 (277 439)	877 189 (277 440)	BBG
477 190 (277 441)	877 190 (277 442)	BBG
477 191 (277 443)	877 191 (277 444)	BBG
477 192 (277 445)	877 192 (277 446)	BBG
477 193 (277 447)	877 193 (277 448)	BBG
477 194 (277 449)	877 194 (277 450)	BBG
477 195 (277 451)	877 195 (277 452)	BBG
477 196 (277 453)	877 196 (277 454)	BBG
477 197 (277 003)	877 197 (277 004)	(Z)
477 198 (277 027)	877 198 (277 028)	(Z)
477 199 (277 033)	877 199 (277 034)	(Z)
477 200 (277 047)	877 200 (277 048)	(Z)
477 201 (277 051)	877 201 (277 052)	(Z)

477 202 (277 063)	877 202 (277 064)	(Z)
477 203 (277 065)	877 203 (277 066)	(Z)
477 204 (277 069)	877 204 (277 070)	(Z)
477 205 (277 073)	877 205 (277 074)	(Z)
477 206 (277 087)	877 206 (277 088)	(Z)
477 207 (277 103)	877 207 (277 104)	(Z)
477 208 (277 201)	877 208 (277 202)	(Z)
477 601 (277 403)	877 601 (277 404)	BBG
477 602 (277 405)	877 602 (277 406)	BBG
477 603 (277 407)	877 603 (277 408)	BBG
477 604 (277 409)	877 604 (277 410)	BBG
477 605 (277 413)	877 605 (277 414)	BBG
477 606 (277 415)	877 606 (277 416)	BBG
477 607 (277 419)	877 607 (277 420)	BBG
477 608 (277 421)	877 608 (277 422)	BBG

CLASS 478   2-CAR UNITS

Built: 1925-26.
System: 800 V dc third rail.
Electrical Equipment:
Continuous Rating: 460 kW.
Wheel Arrangements: Bo-Bo + 2-2
Weight: 78.20 tonnes.
Length: 35.960 m.
Maximum Speed: 80 km/h.
Seats:
Note: Power and trailer cars are coupled in pairs. Four pairs are coupled together to form the normal train formation. These cars are used for departmental services and also as baggage cars.

478 001 (278 001)	878 002 (278 002)	BBW
478 003 (278 003)		BBW
478 004 (278 005)	878 004 (278 006)	BBF
478 005 (278 007)	878 005 (278 008)	BBF
478 006 (278 101)	878 006 (278 102)	BBF
478 007 (278 103)	878 007 (278 104)	BBF
478 008 (278 105)		BBS
478 009 (278 109)	878 009 (278 110)	BBW
478 010 (278 111)	878 010 (278 112)	BBW
478 011 (278 113)	878 011 (278 114)	BBW

CLASS 479.2
SINGLE UNITS

Built: 1923. Rebuilt 1981 by DR Schöneweide Works.
System: 500 V dc overhead.
Electrical Equipment:
Continuous Rating: 120 kW.
Wheel Arrangements: Bo.
Weight: 14.40 tonnes.
Length: 11.500 m.
Maximum Speed: 50 km/h.
Seats: 24.
Note: These vehicles work between Lichtenhain and Cursdorf.

479 201 (279 201)	US	479 205 (279 205)	US
479 203 (279 203)	US		

CLASSES 479.6/879.6
2-CAR UNITS

Built: 1930 by Hannoversche. Rebuilt 1982 by DR Sch"neweide Works.
System: 600 V dc overhead.
Electrical Equipment:
Continuous Rating: 120 kW per power car.
Wheel Arrangements: Bo + 2.
Weight: 22.70 tonnes (Power Car); ??? (trailer)
Length: 14.300 m. (Power Car); ??? (trailer).
Maximum Speed: 50 km/h.
Seats: 30 (Power Car); ??? (trailer).
Notes: These vehicles work the line between Müncheberg and Buckow and are scheduled for withdrawal at the commencement of the Summer 1992 timetable when the line is dieselised.

479 601 (279 001)	879 601 (279 002)	BB
479 602 (279 003)	879 602 (279 004)	BB
479 603 (279 005)	879 603 (279 006)	BB

CLASSES 485/885
2-CAR HALF UNITS

Built: 1987 onwards by LEW.
System: 800 V dc third rail.
Electrical Equipment: LEW.
Continuous Rating: 600 kW per power car.
Wheel Arrangements: Bo-Bo + 2-2
Weight: 60 tonnes per two car set.

Length: 36.000 per two car set.
Maximum Speed: 90 km/h.
Seats: 102S per two car set.
Note: Power and trailer cars are coupled in pairs. Four pairs are coupled together to form the normal train formation. Vehicles numbered 475.6 may operate as two car sets as the trailer is a driving trailer.

485 005 (270 009)	885 005 (270 010)	BBF
485 006 (270 011)	885 006 (270 012)	BBF
485 007 (270 013)	885 007 (270 014)	BBF
485 008 (270 015)	885 008 (270 016)	BBF
485 009 (270 017)	885 009 (270 018)	BBF
485 010 (270 019)	885 010 (270 020)	BBF
485 011 (270 021)	885 011 (270 022)	BBF
485 012 (270 023)	885 012 (270 024)	BBF
485 013 (270 025)	885 013 (270 026)	BBF
485 014 (270 027)	885 014 (270 028)	BBF
485 015 (270 029)	885 015 (270 030)	BBF
485 016 (270 031)	885 016 (270 032)	BBG
485 017 (270 033)	885 017 (270 034)	BBF
485 018 (270 035)	885 018 (270 036)	BBF
485 019 (270 037)	885 019 (270 038)	BBF
485 020 (270 039)	885 020 (270 040)	BBF
485 021 (270 041)	885 021 (270 042)	BBF
485 022 (270 043)	885 022 (270 044)	BBF
485 023 (270 045)	885 023 (270 046)	BBF
485 024 (270 047)	885 024 (270 048)	BBF
485 025 (270 049)	885 025 (270 050)	BBF
485 026 (270 051)	885 026 (270 052)	BBF
485 027 (270 053)	885 027 (270 054)	BBF
485 028 (270 055)	885 028 (270 056)	BBF
485 029 (270 057)	885 029 (270 058)	BBF
485 030 (270 059)	885 030 (270 060)	BBF
485 031 (270 061)	885 031 (270 062)	BBF
485 032 (270 063)	885 032 (270 064)	BBF
485 033 (270 065)	885 033 (270 066)	BBF
485 034 (270 067)	885 034 (270 068)	BBF
485 035 (270 069)	885 035 (270 070)	BBG
485 036 (270 071)	885 036 (270 072)	BBG
485 037 (270 073)	885 037 (270 074)	BBF
485 038 (270 075)	885 038 (270 076)	BBF
485 039 (270 077)	885 039 (270 078)	BBG
485 040 (270 079)	885 040 (270 080)	BBG
485 041 (270 081)	885 041 (270 082)	BBG

485 042 (270 083)	885 042 (270 084)	BBF
485 043 (270 085)	885 043 (270 086)	BBG
485 044 (270 087)	885 044 (270 088)	BBG
485 045 (270 089)	885 045 (270 090)	BBG
485 046 (270 091)	885 046 (270 092)	BBG
485 047 (270 093)	885 047 (270 094)	BBG
485 048 (270 095)	885 048 (270 096)	BBG
485 049 (270 097)	885 049 (270 098)	BBG
485 050 (270 099)	885 050 (270 100)	BBG
485 051 (270 101)	885 051 (270 102)	BBG
485 052 (270 103)	885 052 (270 104)	BBG
485 053 (270 105)	885 053 (270 106)	BBG
485 054 (270 107)	885 054 (270 108)	BBG
485 055 (270 109)	885 055 (270 110)	BBG
485 056 (270 111)	885 056 (270 112)	BBG
485 057 (270 113)	885 057 (270 114)	BBG
485 058 (270 115)	885 058 (270 116)	BBG
485 059 (270 117)	885 059 (270 118)	BBG
485 060 (270 119)	885 060 (270 120)	BBG
485 061 (270 121)	885 061 (270 122)	BBG
485 062 (270 123)	885 062 (270 124)	BBG
485 063 (270 125)	885 063 (270 126)	BBG
485 064 (270 127)	885 064 (270 128)	BBG
485 065 (270 129)	885 065 (270 130)	BBG
485 066 (270 131)	885 066 (270 132)	BBG
485 067 (270 133)	885 067 (270 134)	BBG
485 068 (270 135)	885 068 (270 136)	BBG
485 069 (270 137)	885 069 (270 138)	BBG
485 070 (270 139)	885 070 (270 140)	BBG
485 071 (270 141)	885 071 (270 142)	BBG
485 072 (270 143)	885 072 (270 144)	BBG
485 073 (270 145)	885 073 (270 146)	BBG
485 074 (270 147)	885 074 (270 148)	BBG
485 075 (270 149)	885 075 (270 150)	BBG
485 076 (270 151)	885 076 (270 152)	BBG
485 077 (270 153)	885 077 (270 154)	BBG
485 078 (270 155)	885 078 (270 156)	BBG
485 079 (270 157)	885 079 (270 158)	BBG
485 080 (270 159)	885 080 (270 160)	BBG
485 081 (270 161)	885 081 (270 162)	BBG
485 082 (270 163)	885 082 (270 164)	BBG
485 083 (270 165)	885 083 (270 166)	BBG
485 084 (270 167)	885 084 (270 168)	BBG
485 085 (270 169)	885 085 (270 170)	BBG

485 086 (270 171)	885 086 (270 172)	BBG
485 087 (270 173)	885 087 (270 174)	BBG
485 088 (270 175)	885 088 (270 176)	BBG
485 089 (270 177)	885 089 (270 178)	BBG
485 090 (270 179)	885 090 (270 180)	BBG
485 091 (270 181)	885 091 (270 182)	BBG
485 092 (270 183)	885 092 (270 184)	BBG
485 093 (270 185)	885 093 (270 186)	BBG
485 094 (270 187)	885 094 (270 188)	BBG
485 095 (270 189)	885 095 (270 190)	BBG
485 096	885 096	BBG
485 097	885 097	BBG
485 098	885 098	BBG
485 099	885 099	BBG
485 100	885 100	BBG
485 101	885 101	BBG
485 102	885 102	BBG
485 103	885 103	BBG
485 104	885 104	BBG
485 105	885 105	BBG
485 106	885 106	BBG
485 107	885 107	BBG
485 108	885 108	BBG
485 109	885 109	BBG
485 110	885 110	BBG
485 111	885 111	BBG
485 112	885 112	
485 113	885 113	
485 114	885 114	
485 115	885 115	
485 116	885 116	
485 117	885 117	
485 118	885 118	
485 119	885 119	
485 120	885 120	
485 121	885 121	
485 122	885 122	
485 123	885 123	
485 124	885 124	
485 125	885 125	
485 126	885 126	
485 127	885 127	
485 128	885 128	
485 129	885 129	

485 130	885 130
485 131	885 131
485 132	885 132
485 133	885 133
485 134	885 134
485 135	885 135
485 136	885 136
485 137	885 137
485 138	885 138
485 139	885 139
485 140	885 140
485 141	885 141
485 142	885 142
485 143	885 143
485 144	885 144
485 145	885 145
485 146	885 146
485 147	885 147
485 148	885 148
485 149	885 149
485 150	885 150
485 151	885 151
485 152	885 152
485 153	885 153

CLASS 491   SINGLE UNIT

Built: 1936 by Fuchs.
System: 15 kV ac 16.67 Hz ac overhead.
Electrical Equipment: AEG.
Continuous Rating: 350 kW.
Wheel Arrangement: Bo-2.
Weight: 45.40 tonnes.
Length: 20.600 m.
Maximum Speed: 120 km/h.
Seats: 72.

491 001 MH4

BATTERY ELECTRIC MULTIPLE UNITS

CLASSES 515   SINGLE UNIT

Built: 1959-63 by DWM/MAN/O & K/Rathgeber.
Batteries: 520 kWh.
Electrical Equipment: AFA/DWM/Schaltbau/Siemens
Continuous Rating: 200 kW.
Wheel Arrangement: Bo-2.
Weight: 57 tonnes.
Length: 23.400 m.
Maximum Speed: 100 km/h.
Seats: 6F, 59S. (* 19F, 40S)
Notes: All equipped for one person operation (with automatic doors).

515 516 KM	515 549 EWAN	515 605 EWAN
515 520 KM	515 551 EWAN	515 608 EWAN
515 522 KM	515 554 EWAN	515 611 EWAN
515 525 KM	515 556 EWAN	515 616 KM
515 526 KM	515 557 EWAN	515 633 EWAN
515 528 EWAN	515 566 EWAN	515 636 EWAN
515 529 EWAN	515 567 KM	515 643* EWAN
515 530 KM	515 580 EWAN	515 645* EWAN
515 536 EWAN	515 591* EWAN	
515 548 EWAN	515 604 KM	

DEPARTMENTAL VEHICLES

CLASS 701   OHL MAINTENANCE CARS

Built: 1954-64 by MBB/Rathgeber.
Engine: Two Büssing of 110 kW each.
Transmission: Mechanical.
Wheel Arrangement: A-A.
Weight: 24.60 tonnes.
Length: 13.950 m.
Maximum Speed: 90 km/h.

701 001 TK	701 005 RM	701 009 HH
701 002 ESIE	701 006 RK	701 010 MH1
701 003 EHM	701 007 HG	701 011 RSI
701 004 RM	701 008 FK	701 012 RK

▲ 515 604 awaits departure from Kaarst with the 1649 to Neuss 30.01.92   (S. McNally)

▼ 701 071 at Bw Singen 21.09.89   (R.G. Morris)

701 013 MA	701 064 MIH	701 110 EOB
701 014 FG	701 065 MFL	701 111 TK
701 015 FF2	701 066 NN1	701 112 EDO
701 016 RM	701 067 NN1	701 113 MH1
701 017 EHM	701 068 SSH	701 114 EHM
701 018 KK	701 069 TK	701 116 EOB
701 019 KW	701 070 TK	701 117 MIH
701 020 FD	701 071 RO	701 118 HO
701 021 RM	701 072 FK	701 119 HA
701 022 NN1	701 073 EOB	701 120 EHM
701 023 HG	701 074 FD	701 121 HO
701 024 FK	701 075 HG	701 122 TK
701 025 TK	701 076 HH	701 126 HO
701 026 EOB	701 077 HB	701 127 HB
701 027 MH1	701 078 HBS	701 128 RSI
701 028 MMF	701 079 HB	701 130 AH4
701 029 NWH	701 080 HH	701 139 EHM
701 030 NRH	701 081 HE	701 140 EDO
701 031 NRH	701 082 HB	701 141 EOB
701 032 TH	701 083 HH	701 142 FF2
701 033 TK	701 084 KKR	701 143 FD
701 034 HG	701 085 KKR	701 144 MA
701 035 FD	701 086 RM	701 145 EDO
701 036 KK	701 087 KK	701 146 HH
701 037 MA	701 088 HO	701 147 STR
701 038 EDO	701 089 NN1	701 151 TH
701 039 FF2	701 090 HH	701 152 TH
701 040 KK	701 091 SSH	701 153 TK
701 043 NN1	701 095 AH4	701 154 NWH
701 044 KK	701 096 AH4	701 155 STR
701 045 FFU	701 097 AH4	701 156 RM
701 046 HO	701 098 FK	701 157 EHM
701 047 FFU	701 099 FK	701 158 MH1
701 048 KW	701 100 FK	701 159 MH1
701 051 ESIE	701 101 HBS	701 160 KK
701 052 EOB	701 102 FF2	701 161 HA
701 053 HH	701 103 FF2	701 162 HB
701 054 HG	701 104 FG	701 165 MMF
701 058 KKR	701 105 FD	701 166 TK
701 059 SKL	701 106 KK	701 167 EDO
701 060 KK	701 107 KK	701 168 RO
701 062 MA	701 108 KK	701 169 EHM
701 063 FK	701 109 RM	701 170 HBS

▲ 702 132 at Bw Stuttgart Kornwestheim 24.07.88   (B.A. Hawkins)

▼ 704 004 at Bw Würzburg 19.07.88   (B.A. Hawkins)

CLASS 702   OHL MAINTENANCE CARS

Built: 1954-64 by MBB/Rathgeber as class 701. One engine removed 1967.
Engine: Büssing of 110 kW.
Transmission: Mechanical.
Wheel Arrangement: 1-A.
Weight: 21.80 tonnes.
Length: 13.950 m.
Maximum Speed: 90 km/h.

702 042 KW	702 125 MH1	702 137 MA
702 049 KW	702 129 NN1	702 138 NRH
702 050 KW	702 131 RHL	702 148 RK
702 055 RF	702 132 FFU	702 149 TK
702 056 RF	702 133 TK	702 150 NN1
702 115 MH1	702 134 KW	702 163 SSH
702 123 MH1	702 135 HG	702 164 AH4
702 124 MH1	702 136 MH1	

CLASS 704   OHL MAINTENANCE CARS

Built: 1977-78 by LHB.
Engine: MaK of 260 kW.
Transmission: Hydraulic.
Weight:
Length: 22.500 m.
Maximum Speed: 120 km/h.

704 001 HG	704 003 FK	704 005 FFU
704 002 RM	704 004 NWH	

CLASS 708.0   OHL MAINTENANCE CARS

Built: 1956-58 by Görlitz.
Engine: IFA of 99 kW (* Johannisthal of 111 kW).
Transmission: Mechanical. Strömungsmachinen 4-Speed.
Wheel Arrangment: A-1.
Weight: 26.0 tonnes.
Length: 13.100 m.
Maximum Speed: 70 km/h.

708 001 (188 001) BSN	708 003* (188 003) (Z)
708 002 (188 002) LG	708 006* (188 006) LLS

CLASS 708.2   OHL MAINTENANCE CARS

Built: 1968-69 by Görlitz.
Engine: Johannisthal of 132 kW.
Transmission: Mechanical. Strömungsmaschinen.
Wheel Arrangement: 1A-2.
Weight: 43.0 tonnes.
Length: 19.300 m.
Maximum Speed: 80 km/h.

708 200 (188 200)	CR	708 203 (188 203)	DC
708 201 (188 201)	UE	708 204 (188 204)	BC
708 202 (188 202)	DRI	708 205 (188 205)	LLS

CLASS 708.3   OHL MAINTENANCE CARS

Built: 1987-92 by Görlitz.
Engine: Johannisthal 6VD18/15 AL-2 of 331 kW.
Transmission: Mechanical. Strömungsmaschinen.
Wheel Arrangement: B-2.
Weight: 58.0 tonnes.
Length: 22.400 m.
Maximum Speed: 100 km/h.

708 301 (188 301)	DD	708 318 (188 318)	UE
708 302 (188 302)	LLS	708 319 (188 319)	BC
708 303 (188 303)	DR	708 320 (188 320)	LLS
708 304 (188 304)	BSN	708 321 (188 321)	DC
708 305 (188 305)	BSN	708 322 (188 322)	BF
708 306 (188 306)	BE	708 323 (188 323)	CA
708 307 (188 307)	CNZ	708 324 (188 324)	LST
708 308 (188 308)	CP	708 325 (188 325)	LLS
708 309 (188 309)	LLS	708 326 (188 326)	CST
708 310 (188 310)	LST	708 327 (188 327)	CHL
708 311 (188 311)	CHL	708 328 (188 328)	BH
708 312 (188 312)	BSG	708 329 (188 329)	DD
708 313 (188 313)	CST	708 330 (188 330)	LST
708 314 (188 314)	CHL	708 331 (188 331)	LLS
708 315 (188 315)	BSN	708 332 (188 332)	CWE
708 316 (188 316)	LLS	708 333 (188 333)	UE
708 317 (188 317)	BSN	708 334 (188 334)	BSN

CLASS 712   TUNNEL INSPECTION UNIT
Built: 1936 by MAN. Converted 1971 from diesel unit VT 38 002.
Engine:
Transmission: Electric.
Wheel Arrangement: B-2.
Weight:
Length: 21.880 m.
Maximum Speed:

712 001 RK

CLASS 715   B-B
Built:
Engine:
Transmission: Hydraulic.
Weight:
Length: 12.000 m.
Maximum Speed:
Notes: Owned by Speno, whose rail grinding train they operate.

715 004 HH   715 005 HH

CLASSES 719/720   RAIL TESTING UNIT
Built: 1974.
Engine:
Transmission:
Weight:
Length:
Maximum Speed:
Notes:

719 001 719 501 720 001 HBS

CLASS 723   RADIO TEST UNIT
Built:
Engine:
Transmission:
Weight:
Length:
Maximum Speed:
Notes:
723 101 (188 101)   BBH

▲ 188 330 (now 708 330) at Bw Stendal 14.04.91   (D. Rowland)

▼ 719 001 + 719 501 + 720 001 stabled at Kirchenlaibach 24.08.87   (N.E. Webster)

CLASS 724   INDUSI TEST CARS

Built: 1952-54 by Uerdingen/Rathgeber/Lüttgens/Orion/WMD.
Engine: Büssing of 110 kW.
Transmission: Mechanical.
Wheel Arrangement: A-1.
Weight: 13.30 tonnes.
Length: 13.265 m (724 003); 13.298 m (724 002).
Maximum Speed: 90 km/h.

724 002 (795 471)   KW   724 003 (795 144)   KW

CLASSES 725/726   TRACK TESTING UNITS

Built: 1959-62 by Uerdingen/MAN/WMD(Class 725); 1974 (Class 726).
Engine: Two Büssing of 110 kW each (Class 725 only).
Transmission: Mechanical.
Wheel Arrangement: Bo + 1-1.
Weight:
Length: 13.950 m.
Maximum Speed: 90 km/h.

725 001 (798 804)	MA	726 001	MA
725 002 (798 676)	FD	726 002	FD
725 003 (798 779)	HBS	726 003	HBS
725 004 (798 674)	KW	726 004	KW
725 005 (798 799)	NN1	726 005	NN1

CLASS 727   CAB SIGNALLING TEST CAR

Built: 1952 by Uerdingen.
Engine: Büssing of 110 kW.
Transmission: Mechanical.
Weight:
Length: 13.265 m.
Maximum Speed: 90 km/h.

727 001 (795 113)   MH1

▲ 724 003 at Köln Hbf depot 25.02.90

(R.G. Morris)

▼ 725 001 and 726 001 at Bw Augsburg 18.07.87

(B.A. Hawkins)

CLASS 728 INDUSI TEST CAR

Built: 1962 by Uerdingen/MAN/WMD. Converted 1985.
Engines: Two Büssing of 110 kW each.
Transmission: Mechanical.
Wheel Arrangement: Bo.
Weight:
Length: 13.950 m.
Maximum Speed: 90 km/h.

728 001 (798 813)   KW

CLASS 732 DE-ICING CAR

Built: 1959-63 by DWM/MAN/O & K/Rathgeber. Converted 1991.
Batteries: 520 kWh.
Electrical Equipment: AFA/DWM/Schaltbau/Siemens.
Continuous Rating: 200 kW.
Wheel Arrangement: Bo-2.
Weight:
Length: 23.400 m.
Maximum Speed: 100 km/h.

732 001 (515 505)   AOP

CLASS 740 S & T TEST CARS

Built: 1959-62 by Uerdingen/MAN/WMD. Converted 1990-92.
Engine: Two Büssing of 110 kW each.
Transmission: Mechanical.
Wheel Arrangement: Bo.
Weight:
Length: 13.950 m.
Maximum Speed: 90 km/h.

740 001 (798 827)	FFU	740 004 (798 735)	
740 002 (798 705)	FK	740 005 (798 693)	
740 003 (798 574)	TK		

750 001 Co-Co

Built: 1965 by Henschel.
System: 15 kV ac 16.67 Hz ac overhead.
Electrical Equipment: Siemens.

▲ 728 001 at Bw Kempten 24.07.88   (B.A. Hawkins)

▼ 750 001 at Bremen 11.05.90   (P. Wormald)

Continuous Rating: 5950 kW.
Weight: 110 tonnes.
Length: 19.50 m.
Maximum Speed: 200 km/h.
Train Heating: Electric (1000 V system).

750 001 (103 001)   AH1

750 003 Co-Co

Built: 1970-74 by Henschel/Krauss-Maffei/Krupp.
System: 15 kV ac 16.67 Hz ac overhead.
Electrical Equipment: Siemens/AEG/BBC.
Continuous Rating: 7440 kW.
Weight: 114 tonnes.
Length: 20.20 m.
Maximum Speed: 200 km/h.
Train Heating: Electric (1000 V system).

750 003 (103 222)   AH1

CLASS 751 Bo-Bo

Built: 1965 by Henschel/Krauss-Maffei/Krupp.
System: 15 kV ac 16.67 Hz ac overhead.
Electrical Equipment: BBC/Siemens/AEG.
Continuous Rating: 3620 kW (4920 hp).
Weight: 84.6 tonnes.
Length: 16.49 m.
Maximum Speed: 150 km/h.
Train Heating: Electric (1000 V system).

751 001 (110 385)   AH1

CLASS 752 Bo-Bo

Built: 1979 by Henschel/Krauss-Maffei/Krupp.
System: 15 kV ac 16.67 Hz ac overhead.
Electrical Equipment: BBC.
Continuous Rating: 5600 kW.
Weight: 83.2 tonnes.
Length: 19.20 m.
Maximum Speed: 200 km/h.

▲ 750 003 leaves Hannover Hbf 18.06.91 (A.J. Marshall)

▼ 752 001 at Minden 23.04.90 (R.G. Morris)

Train Heating: Electric (1000 V system).
Note: 752 005 has been rebuilt as a test bed for the proposed class 121. Revised technical details are not yet available.

752 001 (120 001)	NN2	Nürnberg
752 002 (120 002)	NN2	Fürth
752 003 (120 003)	NN2	
752 004 (120 004)	NN2	
752 005 (120 005)	NN2	

CLASS 753   B-B
Built: 1965 by Krupp.
Engine: Mercedes 16 V 652 TB of 1400 kW at 1500 rpm.
Transmission: Hydraulic. Voith L820brs.
Weight:
Length: 16.40 m (53 ft 10 in).
Maximum Speed: 140 km/h (88 mph).
Train Heating: Not equipped.

753 001 (217 001)	NRH	753 002 (217 002) NRH

ELECTRIC MULTIPLE UNIT TRAILER CARS

CLASS 801.0   ICE TRAILER FIRST
Built: 1990-92 by Duewag.
Wheel Arrangement: 2-2.
Weight: 52.80 tonnes.
Length: 26.400 m.
Maximum Speed: 280 km/h.
Seats: 48F.

801 001 AH1	801 011 AH1	801 021 AH1
801 002 AH1	801 012 AH1	801 022 AH1
801 003 AH1	801 013 AH1	801 023 AH1
801 004 AH1	801 014 AH1	801 024 AH1
801 005 AH1	801 015 AH1	801 025 AH1
801 006 AH1	801 016 AH1	801 026 AH1
801 007 AH1	801 017 AH1	801 027 AH1
801 008 AH1	801 018 AH1	801 028 AH1
801 009 AH1	801 019 AH1	801 029 AH1
801 010 AH1	801 020 AH1	801 030 AH1

801 031 AH1	801 049 AH1	801 067 AH1
801 032 AH1	801 050 AH1	801 068 AH1
801 033 AH1	801 051 AH1	801 069 AH1
801 034 AH1	801 052 AH1	801 070 AH1
801 035 AH1	801 053 AH1	801 071 AH1
801 036 AH1	801 054 AH1	801 072 AH1
801 037 AH1	801 055 AH1	801 073 AH1
801 038 AH1	801 056 AH1	801 074 AH1
801 039 AH1	801 057 AH1	801 075 AH1
801 040 AH1	801 058 AH1	801 076 AH1
801 041 AH1	801 059 AH1	801 077 AH1
801 042 AH1	801 060 AH1	801 078 AH1
801 043 AH1	801 061 AH1	801 079 AH1
801 044 AH1	801 062 AH1	801 080 AH1
801 045 AH1	801 063 AH1	801 081 AH1
801 046 AH1	801 064 AH1	801 082 AH1
801 047 AH1	801 065 AH1	
801 048 AH1	801 066 AH1	

CLASS 801.4　　　　　　　ICE TRAILER FIRST

Built: 1990-92 by Waggon Union.
Wheel Arrangement: 2-2.
Weight: 52.80 tonnes.
Length: 26.400 m.
Maximum Speed: 280 km/h.
Seats: 48F.

801 401 AH1	801 409 AH1	801 417 AH1
801 402 AH1	801 410 AH1	801 418 AH1
801 403 AH1	801 411 AH1	801 419 AH1
801 404 AH1	801 412 AH1	801 420 AH1
801 405 AH1	801 413 AH1	801 421 AH1
801 406 AH1	801 414 AH1	801 422 AH1
801 407 AH1	801 415 AH1	801 423 AH1
801 408 AH1	801 416 AH1	

CLASS 801.8　　　　　　　ICE TRAILER FIRST

Built: 1990-92 by Waggon Union.
Wheel Arrangement: 2-2.
Weight: 52.80 tonnes.
Length: 26.400 m.
Maximum Speed: 280 km/h.
Seats: 48F.

801 801 AH1	801 815 AH1	801 829 AH1
801 802 AH1	801 816 AH1	801 830 AH1
801 803 AH1	801 817 AH1	801 831 AH1
801 804 AH1	801 818 AH1	801 832 AH1
801 805 AH1	801 819 AH1	801 833 AH1
801 806 AH1	801 820 AH1	801 834 AH1
801 807 AH1	801 821 AH1	801 835 AH1
801 808 AH1	801 822 AH1	801 836 AH1
801 809 AH1	801 823 AH1	801 837 AH1
801 810 AH1	801 824 AH1	801 838 AH1
801 811 AH1	801 825 AH1	801 839 AH1
801 812 AH1	801 826 AH1	801 840 AH1
801 813 AH1	801 827 AH1	801 841 AH1
801 814 AH1	801 828 AH1	

CLASS 802.0   ICE TRAILER SECOND

Built: 1990-92 by Duewag/LHB.
Wheel Arrangement: 2-2.
Weight: 52.80 tonnes.
Length: 26.400 m.
Maximum Speed: 280 km/h.
Seats: 66S.

802 001 AH1	802 022 AH1	802 043 AH1
802 002 AH1	802 023 AH1	802 044 AH1
802 003 AH1	802 024 AH1	802 045 AH1
802 004 AH1	802 025 AH1	802 046 AH1
802 005 AH1	802 026 AH1	802 047 AH1
802 006 AH1	802 027 AH1	802 048 AH1
802 007 AH1	802 028 AH1	802 049 AH1
802 008 AH1	802 029 AH1	802 050 AH1
802 009 AH1	802 030 AH1	802 051 AH1
802 010 AH1	802 031 AH1	802 052 AH1
802 011 AH1	802 032 AH1	802 053 AH1
802 012 AH1	802 033 AH1	802 054 AH1
802 013 AH1	802 034 AH1	802 055 AH1
802 014 AH1	802 035 AH1	802 056 AH1
802 015 AH1	802 036 AH1	802 057 AH1
802 016 AH1	802 037 AH1	802 058 AH1
802 017 AH1	802 038 AH1	802 059 AH1
802 018 AH1	802 039 AH1	802 060 AH1
802 019 AH1	802 040 AH1	802 061 AH1
802 020 AH1	802 041 AH1	802 062 AH1
802 021 AH1	802 042 AH1	802 063 AH1

802 064 AH1	802 071 AH1	802 078 AH1
802 065 AH1	802 072 AH1	802 079 AH1
802 066 AH1	802 073 AH1	802 080 AH1
802 067 AH1	802 074 AH1	802 081 AH1
802 068 AH1	802 075 AH1	802 082 AH1
802 069 AH1	802 076 AH1	
802 070 AH1	802 077 AH1	

CLASS 802.3   ICE TRAILER SECOND

Built: 1990-92 by LHB/MBB/MAN.
Wheel Arrangement: 2-2.
Weight: 52.80 tonnes.
Length: 26.400 m.
Maximum Speed: 280 km/h.
Seats: 66S.

802 301 AH1	802 329 AH1	802 357 AH1
802 302 AH1	802 330 AH1	802 358 AH1
802 303 AH1	802 331 AH1	802 359 AH1
802 304 AH1	802 332 AH1	802 360 AH1
802 305 AH1	802 333 AH1	802 361 AH1
802 306 AH1	802 334 AH1	802 362 AH1
802 307 AH1	802 335 AH1	802 363 AH1
802 308 AH1	802 336 AH1	802 364 AH1
802 309 AH1	802 337 AH1	802 365 AH1
802 310 AH1	802 338 AH1	802 366 AH1
802 311 AH1	802 339 AH1	802 367 AH1
802 312 AH1	802 340 AH1	802 368 AH1
802 313 AH1	802 341 AH1	802 369 AH1
802 314 AH1	802 342 AH1	802 370 AH1
802 315 AH1	802 343 AH1	802 371 AH1
802 316 AH1	802 344 AH1	802 372 AH1
802 317 AH1	802 345 AH1	802 373 AH1
802 318 AH1	802 346 AH1	802 374 AH1
802 319 AH1	802 347 AH1	802 375 AH1
802 320 AH1	802 348 AH1	802 376 AH1
802 321 AH1	802 349 AH1	802 377 AH1
802 322 AH1	802 350 AH1	802 378 AH1
802 323 AH1	802 351 AH1	802 379 AH1
802 324 AH1	802 352 AH1	802 380 AH1
802 325 AH1	802 353 AH1	802 381 AH1
802 326 AH1	802 354 AH1	802 382 AH1
802 327 AH1	802 355 AH1	802 383 AH1
802 328 AH1	802 356 AH1	802 384 AH1

802 385 AH1	802 391 AH1	802 397 AH1
802 386 AH1	802 392 AH1	802 398 AH1
802 387 AH1	802 393 AH1	802 399 AH1
802 388 AH1	802 394 AH1	802 400 AH1
802 389 AH1	802 395 AH1	
802 390 AH1	802 396 AH1	

CLASS 802.6   ICE TRAILER SECOND

Built: 1990-92 by MBB.
Wheel Arrangement: 2-2.
Weight: 52.80 tonnes.
Length: 26.400 m.
Maximum Speed: 280 km/h.
Seats: 66S.

802 601 AH1	802 615 AH1	802 629 AH1
802 602 AH1	802 616 AH1	802 630 AH1
802 603 AH1	802 617 AH1	802 631 AH1
802 604 AH1	802 618 AH1	802 632 AH1
802 605 AH1	802 619 AH1	802 633 AH1
802 606 AH1	802 620 AH1	802 634 AH1
802 607 AH1	802 621 AH1	802 635 AH1
802 608 AH1	802 622 AH1	802 636 AH1
802 609 AH1	802 623 AH1	802 637 AH1
802 610 AH1	802 624 AH1	802 638 AH1
802 611 AH1	802 625 AH1	802 639 AH1
802 612 AH1	802 626 AH1	802 640 AH1
802 613 AH1	802 627 AH1	802 641 AH1
802 614 AH1	802 628 AH1	

CLASS 802.8   ICE TRAILER SECOND

Built: 1990-92 by MBB/MAN.
Wheel Arrangement: 2-2.
Weight: 52.80 tonnes.
Length: 26.400 m.
Maximum Speed: 280 km/h.
Seats: 66S.

802 801 AH1	802 808 AH1	802 815 AH1
802 802 AH1	802 809 AH1	802 816 AH1
802 803 AH1	802 810 AH1	802 817 AH1
802 804 AH1	802 811 AH1	802 818 AH1
802 805 AH1	802 812 AH1	802 819 AH1
802 806 AH1	802 813 AH1	802 820 AH1
802 807 AH1	802 814 AH1	

802 821 AH1	802 828 AH1	802 835 AH1
802 822 AH1	802 829 AH1	802 836 AH1
802 823 AH1	802 830 AH1	802 837 AH1
802 824 AH1	802 831 AH1	802 838 AH1
802 825 AH1	802 832 AH1	802 839 AH1
802 826 AH1	802 833 AH1	802 840 AH1
802 827 AH1	802 834 AH1	802 841 AH1

CLASS 803   ICE SPECIAL TRAILER SECOND

Built: 1990-92 by Duewag.
Wheel Arrangement: 2-2.
Weight: 53.60 tonnes.
Length: 26.400 m.
Maximum Speed: 280 km/h.
Seats: 39S + 4 seat conference room.

803 001 AH1	803 015 AH1	803 029 AH1
803 002 AH1	803 016 AH1	803 030 AH1
803 003 AH1	803 017 AH1	803 031 AH1
803 004 AH1	803 018 AH1	803 032 AH1
803 005 AH1	803 019 AH1	803 033 AH1
803 006 AH1	803 020 AH1	803 034 AH1
803 007 AH1	803 021 AH1	803 035 AH1
803 008 AH1	803 022 AH1	803 036 AH1
803 009 AH1	803 023 AH1	803 037 AH1
803 010 AH1	803 024 AH1	803 038 AH1
803 011 AH1	803 025 AH1	803 039 AH1
803 012 AH1	803 026 AH1	803 040 AH1
803 013 AH1	803 027 AH1	803 041 AH1
803 014 AH1	803 028 AH1	

CLASS 804   ICE RESTAURANT/BAR

Built: 1990-92 by Waggon Union.
Wheel Arrangement: 2-2.
Weight: 58.20 tonnes.
Length: 26.400 m.
Maximum Speed: 280 km/h.
Seats: 24 restaurant seats + bar seating.

804 001 AH1	804 006 AH1	804 011 AH1
804 002 AH1	804 007 AH1	804 012 AH1
804 003 AH1	804 008 AH1	804 013 AH1
804 004 AH1	804 009 AH1	804 014 AH1
804 005 AH1	804 010 AH1	804 015 AH1

804 016 AH1	804 025 AH1	804 034 AH1
804 017 AH1	804 026 AH1	804 035 AH1
804 018 AH1	804 027 AH1	804 036 AH1
804 019 AH1	804 028 AH1	804 037 AH1
804 020 AH1	804 029 AH1	804 038 AH1
804 021 AH1	804 030 AH1	804 039 AH1
804 022 AH1	804 031 AH1	804 040 AH1
804 023 AH1	804 032 AH1	804 041 AH1
804 024 AH1	804 033 AH1	

BATTERY UNIT TRAILERS

CLASS 815   BATTERY UNIT TRAILERS

Built: 1956-64 by O & K/Rathgeber.
Wheel Arrangement: 2-2.
Weight: 23 tonnes.
Length: 23.400 m.
Maximum Speed: 100 km/h.
Seats: 81S.
Notes: All equipped for one person operation (with automatic doors).

815 617 EWAN	815 696 EWAN	815 713 KM
815 672 EWAN	815 697 EWAN	815 807 KM
815 690 KM	815 706 EWAN	
815 691 KM	815 711 KM	

142

RAIL EUROPE

PO BOX 1, ALLERTON, BRADFORD, BD15 9BU, ENGLAND

Quality tours for rail enthusiasts to all countries in Europe.

Our 1992 programme includes tours to France, The Netherlands, Belgium, Germany, Luxembourg and Poland.

Depot and Works visits arranged, lineside photography opportunities etc. Small, convivial groups with tours planned to suit the individual needs of the participants. Tailor made tours can also be arranged to suit all small parties.

Send (SAE please) for details of our exciting programme.

(Membership from only £5.00 per annum)

1968   **1992**

RAIL EUROPE

25 YEARS OF EUROPEAN TOURS, PROVIDING MORE THAN JUST A TWINKLE OF EXPERTISE.